The essays and poems in this anthology are nonfiction and creative nonfiction. In some cases, names have been changed.

Direct inquiries to skminer@nutshellmediagroup.com

Nutshell Media Group LLC
P. O. Box 784
Wilsonville, OR 97070

www.nutshellmediagroup.com

The Narcissist's Playbook
Paperback ISBN 978-0-692-92197-5

Cover design by Sarah Miner. Cover art is based on an acrylic on canvas painting, "Despair", by anonymous. Interior art photo "Stet" submitted by J. Kathleen Marcus. Interior design by Sarah Miner.

The Narcissist's Playbook

Edited by S. K. Miner and J. Kathleen Marcus

TABLE OF CONTENTS

Like many great works of art produced mostly by women, this book started with two friends commiserating over shared experience. Sarah and I (Jake) were both extricating ourselves from relationships with men who exhibited similar behaviors. These behaviors made us both hunger for a friend to say, "No, it isn't you. You aren't insane."

In discussing my relationship with my own therapist she suggested my then significant other was a "narcissist." I was a bit confused. Isn't a narcissist someone obsessed with their own appearance? Doesn't it derive from the mythic Narcissus who was trapped staring at his own reflection in the water? *Well,* she told me, *as a clinical matter, no. There is a diagnosis.* And she pulled out her Diagnostic and Statistical Manual of Mental Disorders (DSM), and read the diagnostic criteria aloud to me. I will excerpt the relevant (to this book) portions.

A. Significant impairments in personality functioning manifest by:

1. Impairments in self functioning (a or b):

a. Identity: Excessive reference to others for self-definition and self-esteem regulation; exaggerated self-appraisal may be inflated or deflated, or vacillate between extremes; emotional regulation mirrors fluctuations in self-esteem.

b. Self-direction: Goal-setting is based on gaining approval from others; personal standards are unreasonably high in order to see oneself as exceptional, or too low based on a sense of entitlement; often unaware of own motivations.

AND

2. Impairments in interpersonal functioning (a or b):

a. Empathy: Impaired ability to recognize or identify with the feelings and needs of others; excessively attuned to reactions of others, but only if perceived as relevant to self; over- or underestimate of own effect on others.

b. Intimacy: Relationships largely superficial and exist to serve self-esteem regulation; mutuality constrained by little genuine interest in others' experiences and predominance of a need for personal gain

B. Pathological personality traits in the following domain:

1. Antagonism, characterized by:

a. Grandiosity: Feelings of entitlement, either overt or covert; self-centeredness; firmly holding to the belief that one is better than others; condescending toward others.

b. Attention seeking: Excessive attempts to attract and be the focus of the attention of others; admiration seeking.
C. The impairments in personality functioning and the individual's personality trait expression are relatively stable across time and consistent across situations.
D. The impairments in personality functioning and the individual's personality trait expression are not better understood as normative for the individual's developmental stage or socio-cultural environment.
E. The impairments in personality functioning and the individual's personality trait expression are not solely due to the direct physiological effects of a substance (e.g., a drug of abuse, medication) or a general medical condition (e.g., severe head trauma).[1]

Now the DSM is a book for mental health professionals. It should probably have a "do not try this at home" warning label because you can find yourself pathologizing your behavior and that of everyone you know. Without my now former significant other in the room, my psychologist was not diagnosing him. *The DSM is not a toy.*

We as editors also want to make abundantly clear that we are not mental health professionals and do not know if the people written about were ever diagnosed with narcissistic personality disorder. I put this piece of the diagnostic criteria (and diagnosing is far more complicated than recognizing criteria in someone else) here so I can better share my own "aha" moment, and the "omg" moment when I read the criteria to Sarah, along with what led to the extraordinary relief that we were not crazy. We could begin to recover from the damage of these relationships by saying to ourselves, with at least a small degree of confidence, "it's not me, it's him."

That being said, a common theme running through this book is "well maybe a little bit it is me" in a response to cries of "why me?" I can now openly acknowledge that I am attracted to narcissists (using a loose definition vaguely based on the DSM). And/or that I behave in a way that attracts them to me. Regardless, I don't see an abusive behavior and run for the hills. I am always ready to believe that the failing is mine and that is my problem. I'm working on it. Promise.

Another term important to understanding the relationships the authors present in this book is "gas lighting." The term comes from a 1944 film Gaslight (based on an earlier less famous play) starring Ingrid Bergman and Charles Boyer. The plot involves a husband slowly creating situations that make his wife feel that she is going insane: footsteps in the attic only she can hear, objects gone missing and then found mysteriously in her purse.

An important element in the success of the husband's tricks is that he has isolated her in the house and away from all her friends and acquaintances. This behavior is now recognized as a form of emotional abuse very common in domestic violence and "gas lighting" has made its way into common parlance (even though I may be among the few who has actually seen the film).

Perhaps the most emotionally destructive aspect of being in a relationship with someone who exhibits these behaviors and uses these tricks, is that you stop being able to see the world through your own eyes. Your abuser (and the people we write about in this book are or were abusers) becomes the lens through which you view the world. Through that lens you are weak, wrong, inadequate, always at fault. Seeing yourself only as your abuser sees you also involves always hearing his voice in your head.

You judge yourself as he judges you. You feel fear when you think you have wandered from the path he insists you stay on – even if it involves a book you are reading, a meal you have prepared, or how you have placed the toilet paper roll.

Abusers of this sort are not all men, as a few of our authors poignantly write. My (Jake's) mother was my first abuser and her behaviors fit the bill perfectly.

When Sarah put out the call for submissions for this book, we were flooded with essays, poems, and notes of gratitude. We had inadvertently struck a social nerve. To all our authors – those chosen for inclusion in this book and those not – we send thanks and love for trusting us with your pain.

It was important to us that this book not be simply infuriating and grim. What we hope is that the message of this book is, yes, "it's not me, it's him" but also "I can move on and learn from this." It is our fervent hope we have succeeded in sending both messages clearly.

As for thanks, I (Jake) thank Sarah for putting up with my attempts to run away from this project, and we both thank our (many) children for living through seeing mom in a bad relationship and then having to put up with a touch of neglect while we wrote a book about it.

Sometimes I (Sarah) pushed this project forward. Other times it pushed me. I thank Jake for her moral compass and editing expertise. What started as a "Hey, what if..." small collection of personal essays grew to hundreds of pages featuring over sixty contributions by thirty women.

We see ourselves in their work, at various points on the path between the beginning and the recovery, even if the details aren't the same. These women speak with one voice. The experiences are universal.

Sarah Miner and Jake Marcus
July 2017

playbook
noun play·book \-ˌbu̇k\

Simple Definition of playbook
American football : a book that contains descriptions of the different offensive and defensive plays that are used by a team

Full Definition of playbook
1: one or more plays in book form
2: a notebook containing diagrammed football plays
3: a stock of usual tactics or methods <straight from his opponent's political playbook>

Source: Merriam-Webster's Learner's Dictionary

INTRODUCTION
by Jenny Forrester

The Narcissist's Playbook, edited by S.K. Miner and J. Kathleen Marcus, contains definitions, personal accounts, poetry, and prose about living with narcissists. What happened to us? Has anyone else experienced this or am I just missing something? Why is this so difficult to figure out what's wrong? What will become of us in our future relationships?

In all eras, there are narcissistic politicians and governmental regulations and rules that act as gaslighting agents. However, when people who love us and who we also love are gaslighting experts and narcissists, it's hard to get a foothold and live a life worthy of us. We can begin to feel woozy and wrong-headed. We begin to think black is white and up is down and everything turns to haze and flood and quicksand.

In the words of Kathryn Peterson, we see the devastating financial effects of narcissism. Ayesha Fayyaz gives us the poetry of the wounded self, wandering. Mo Daviau, the author of *Every Anxious Wave*, shows us how we fall for narcissists even though we're intelligent and thoughtful and mature. There are stories and poetry to illuminate setting a match for fire to clear out all that gas and to wash the muddy waters clear.

The patriarchy creates particular narratives for women. What we learn from each other's stories is that there are alternatives and that we're not alone. We're not the first ones, and, though we have to craft our own escape raft, the river is there for us to follow.

This book will inspire your continual transformation and give you words to articulate what's happened to you and what can happen for you in your future of healing, solace, and love.

Jenny Forrester

Jenny Forrester has been published in a number of print and online publications, including Seattle's City Arts Magazine, Gobshite Quarter, Nailed Magazine, Hip Mama, The Literary Kitchen, Indiana Review, and Columbia Journal. Her work is included in the *Listen to Your Mother* anthology published by Putnam. She curates the Unchaste Readers Series. Her debut literary memoir *Narrow River, Wide Sky* was published by Hawthorne Books in May 2017.

STEALING DOLLARS, STEALING SENSE: FINANCIAL ABUSE AND NARCISSISTIC FAMILY MEMBERS

by Kathryn Peterson

"He would take our child support checks to pay his child support, even though his kids lived with him and not with his ex wife."

"He started spending our money on other "activities" without my knowledge . . . He was able to empty the bank account without me noticing."

"My mom "tricked" me into signing some forms that would have made her my insurance beneficiary instead of my then- husband."

"He would only allow us to eat chicken, white rice, and green beans for dinner every night because it was what he decided was the most cost effective meal for a family of six."

While physical abuse may leave visible bruises and scars, other types of abuse are much less apparent. Financial abuse, like emotional and mental abuse, can be very insidious. It is often misunderstood, too, even though it is, according to the National Network to End Domestic Violence, all too common, occurring in 98% of abusive relationships. Surveys of survivors report that financial concerns were some of the highest factors in the choice to stay in or to return to the abusive relationship. It makes sense. After all, money is often tied to power, and what better way to gain control than through a person's finances.

Although there has been no definite documented link in psychiatric literature between narcissism and financial abuse, the two do seem to be connected. Jean Twenge, a Professor at San Diego University, says that an increase in narcissism does correlate with an increase in materialism and specifically being well off financially. As Narcissistic Personality Disorder expert Sam Vaknin explains, "money is another word for love in the narcissist's emotional vocabulary. Having been deprived of love early on in the narcissist's childhood, he constantly seeks love substitutes."

For Annette, a visual artist who works in an art gallery in Houston, Texas, the financial abuse was subtle, just like the other ways that her husband covertly controlled her. When the two first married, Annette was 24 and had a bright future in Information Technology. She was making almost $80,000, and things looked good. She married the man who is now her ex-husband and they began to build a life together, a life that was literally "all very picket fences." But the longer she was with her husband, the less personal and financial freedom she had. When she had their only daughter, she ended up doing what many women do, staying home. Sometimes she worked part-time, and sometimes she tended full-time to her child. It was at this point that Annette turned over her finances to him:

> He actually insisted on it, specially after I stopped working full time. I didn't quite trust him, but I gave in. We used to put our direct deposits from work into a joint account, but after I stopped working, he told me that he was just going to put his direct deposits into his personal account. He said that it was just easier in terms of paperwork. So that's when he started spending our money on other "activities" without my knowledge. It was mainly porn and who knows what else. That is also how he was able to empty the bank account without me noticing.

Eventually, Annette began to see that the marriage was eroding, and fast. She realized her husband was having an affair, and that he was becoming increasingly physically and verbally abusive. It was at this point that she decided to leave, but by then, she felt trapped. She had no money because the bank account was empty, and the new car that she had been driving was now under his name. "Again, he said it was just easier that way and it would be less paperwork," Annette says. "So my car was actually under his name."

Even though she wasn't sure how she was going to support herself, Annette chose to leave when her daughter, at that point ten years old, came to her one day and said to her "Mommy, you have to divorce daddy. He's a bad man." Annette packed herself, her daughter, and a few belongings into the car (that was still not in her name), and drove across country, from Wisconsin to Texas. From there, she managed to get control of the car and to divorce her husband, although the divorce process was certainly not easy.

For Oliver, a college instructor now in his early thirties, it was the financial control attempted by his now ex-girlfriend that prompted him to examine the relationship. While there were other kinds of abuse as well (in particular, she threatened the lives of several of Oliver's female friends if they did not stay away from him), he began to question what it would be like if he and the girlfriend actually got married:

> By the middle and end of our relationship, we argued a lot about money and jobs--I wanted her to work (in the future) because I thought with both of us having medical issues, we'd need the money, because insurance wouldn't cover everything.

Granted, most medical costs, but things like co-pay, etc. She had other ideas, wanting to stay home and raise our future children (what a fiasco that would've been) and told me that I had to work to make sure we were provided for, and that I also had to spend time at home and not be a workaholic. At the time, in my mid-twenties, I felt very confused as to what I would be doing for the rest of my life--either working or spending time with family. No matter what I did for her, it seemed like it was expected, not appreciated. "I got you a gift," I'd say. "Of course you did," she'd say. "You're my boyfriend." I wish I could lobotomize that portion of my life, because even today, I'm scarred from that relationship.

Like Oliver, Nicole feels scarred by the financial abuse she endured, but in her case, the abuse came from not a partner, but her stepfather. Nicole, a college student and dance teacher, says that the abuse not only affected her ability to trust in close interpersonal relationships, but also contributed to her eating disorder. In a harrowing description, Nicole relates the story of how her stepfather stole her mother's child support checks and imposed strict regulations about the family's food:

> My mother's first husband after my father was abusive in probably every possible way, although I don't remember much of what my brother and I refer to as, "the hazy years," certain members of my family have clued me in on exactly how horrible he was to her, and to us. We moved into his house, and every time they broke up we had to move out of his house, resulting in us having something like ten moves in three or four years. He would take our child support checks to pay his child support, even though his kids lived with him and not with his ex wife. He wouldn't let our mother give us anything that he couldn't afford to give his children, and he pitched a massive fit at our grandparents' one Christmas because they had gotten my brother and me "too many gifts." He would only allow us to eat chicken, white rice, and green beans for dinner every night because it was what he decided was the most cost effective meal for a family of six. He once made me dig about a half of a cup of canned green beans (literally $.65 at any grocery store) out of the trash, and he made me sit at the table all night until I ate them, because, "Money doesn't grow on fucking trees, Nicole!" This is an incident that I credit with some of the cause of the thirteen year long eating disorder I struggled with well

> into adulthood. One of the last times we moved out he cut the power to the house in August because he wasn't going to pay for us to "open and close the door all damn day" so we had to move everything out in triple degree temps in the dark. into adulthood. One of the last times we moved out he cut the power to the house in August because he wasn't going to pay for us to "open and close the door all damn day" so we had to move everything out in triple degree temps in the dark.

Shay Lynn, a teacher and single mother in Oregon, also experienced financial abuse by a parent, in this case, her mother. She tells how her mother attempted to gain control over Shay Lynn's insurance by an act of willful deception:

> "Once, when I was going in for surgery, my mom "tricked" me into signing some forms that would have made her my beneficiary instead of my then-husband. She just sent me forms with the 'sign here' neon tabs and I was like, 'Oh, what's my mom want?' and should have looked, but it was my mom, right? And then the insurance company called me and asked if I had meant to do that b/c the default of course would have been that my husband would have been my beneficiary." The operative phrase in this case is "but it was my mom, right?" We never expect our parents or our spouses to be our deceivers; we never expect them to do us wrong.

Shay Lynn's story, sadly, is not unique. Christina, a single mother living and working near Houston, Texas, explains how her father stole a trust of "upwards of $30k" that was awarded to her in her parents' divorce: "He told me at 18 I could have it at 21, and at 21 that I could have it when I was 30 or married. When I was 33, he laughed and said that money was gone, that it was never that amount (I received a statement about ten years prior and it was $30K at that time). I later found out that I should have had financial transparency about the money from the age of 14 on, as he was the trustee--but it wasn't a trust fund, it was an award settlement." Like many of the narcissistic abusers who use money to gain power over their victims, Christina's father is wealthy, and uses his wealth to gain leverage over her and others like her:

> The worst part is that he makes upwards of $150K a year (that he reports, anyway) from his own business. It makes it worse that he doesn't need the money AT ALL-- owns 6 houses I know about in Texas, two in Arkansas (one on 40 acres of

and), most are rent houses, and he stole money I have documented belonging to me from the age of 8-- his single mother, sole custodian parent of a child-- zero child support or paternal contact-- on federal welfare programs. Disgusting. Then!! Then he claimed the money was spent on things he bought that-- at the time-- he said were gifts. A couple new tires for my crap car, a $2K crap car when the other crap car died, etc. he said all those things add up. I asked for the proof of the running tab he kept on the debts and said in the future, let me know if I'm being billed in arrears for gifts-- should I expect a bill after Christmas? He didn't speak to me for about 2 months.
He is currently about to pull some shit though, b/c I'm buying my step mother's car. I predict he says to write off the rest I owe ($3K) as a birthday gift, and hold it over my head forever."

The practice of attaching strings to the money that is given seems to be common with financial abusers. Like Christina, Donosa, a freelance writer living in Oregon, has experienced the feeling of being "in-debt" to her parents. Her narcissistic mother, in particular, has made her feel that she owes the family for everything she's gotten. "I fantasize about someday giving my parents a check for $310,000," she says, explaining how badly she wants to feel free of her mother. "The average amount needed to raise a child. Just to wipe myself of debt." Donosa explains that her mother gave her father control of the family finances, partly because her "traditional background allowed it."

According to her, he opened up credit cards, re-mortgaged the house and bought assets using her name too, ruining her credit. But as for me... my parents were basically hypocrites when it came to money. I was taught to budget and make deals, all very good. I wanted an allowance, for my relatives to treat money given to me as investments or loans. Compare that to my brothers, who basically got everything they wanted. They didn't have to negotiate. They either only asked or they just took. Favoritism ruled the day. It's sick, but I very much associate money with power and love now. Hence why I've refused money from my mom as an adult. Money is power. It's the ability to make choices by yourself, for yourself.

Keana, a medical professional living near Galveston, Texas, knows all too well the relationship between money and power and how narcissists use finances to exert their wills. For Keana, the financial abuse began as a result of her good intentions to provide care for her aging parents, and in particular, her father. Keana's father is diabetic and has difficulty walking, even sometimes difficulty sitting upright. He and her mother hired her to be a live-in caregiver for both parents, but in particular her father.

The initial agreement was that she would live rent-free and collect a small stipend for her car, her phone and her other individual expenses, while at the same time she would provide transportation for her father when necessary, in particular for him to go to and from doctor's appointments. She was also tasked with odds and ends around the house and light housekeeping, as well as making sure her father was clean and showered, and if not, she had to help him.

This situation worked for a short period of time, until Keana was in an auto accident and hurt her back. She now has difficulty providing the physical part of her father's caregiving labor, but feels unable to leave the situation, both financially and emotionally. To make matters worse, Keana's brother has come back to challenge her parents' support of her. As Keana says, she can't move out on her own without the funds to do so, and now enough time has passed that her employment history is now spotty. Caring for one's elderly parents, like caring for one's children, does not carry the prestige and work history that she would have gained if she had completed some of the same duties in a hospital or nursing home. Keana feels trapped, unable to move out on her own, and also guilty for not being able to help as much as she would have liked originally. And, as narcissists are likely to do, as Keana has tried to renegotiate due to her own health issues, her parents and brother have continuously shifted the boundaries of what they expect:

> So, on Monday night, my brother and Mom sit me down and yell at me. They say that I don't do anything to pitch in around the house. First of all, my brother is pissed because I have not paid him for the phone. So I owe him $80 because they haven't paid me. Then he even said that I am driving the car around for free, which is not true. So I leave and go sit on the stairs. I can still hear what they are saying about me. My mom goes into her room and comes out with a check for $400. She gives it to me quietly. I take the check, thanking her, and later I find out why she handed it to me out of my brother's view, when I take the check and my phone to the table.
> I had planned to talk, but then my brother cuts in. As usual, he wants to instigate *everything*! So, he says "What's that?" as he points at the check. Then he accusingly asks my mom "Where

> is Your List???" I thought he was talking to me because they have been wanting a detailed list about where my money goes. So, as this should be between my mom and me, I texted my mom a detailed list already. So, I reply to my brother, "I already sent her a list." Then he says, "NO. Her. She has a list for you!"
>
> I look at my mom, and she has nothing to say. As usual, the terms for me "being home to help" my dad have changed yet again. I'm sitting there thinking "*Do you see me? Do you even care?*" My back has been out since two Fridays ago. I picked up my dad from dialysis, and he was so weak after, I had to run inside and get the wheelchair, leaving my dad standing against my car in the driveway. After I got him into the wheelchair, I could not get him inside the house! I was panicking. I did everything to try to get him and the wheelchair into the house, but in the process, I hurt my back again. It was on the mend, until the following Monday. My dad went to take a shower, but I had no idea, and fell when he got out of the shower. I had to pick him up *by myself*, thus hurting my back again!!! So, I have been using a cane to walk around. What do I get??? I get talked about by my brother, and my mom laughs about it too. How is that supposed to make me feel??? Then after all that, my brother brings up other shit. He makes fun of me for never having any money! Really sarcastically though. So without any income because I stay home, how the hell am I supposed to have any money??? Why should they even get mad about that????!!!!! They really should make a contract out of what they expect of me. Then I can sign it, not. Or, better yet, make negotiations. I mean, it's only fair.

It is only fair. But in relationships with narcissists, very little is fair. We may think we are being treated well at first, but in the end, the narcissist will use whatever way he or she can to exert control, and what better way to gain control than over someone's financial resources. This raises the question of what someone who is experiencing abuse can do to get out. Of the seven individuals who generously provided their stories for this essay, six are now out of the financially abusive situations and are healing, even though the legacy of the abuse remains. Keana, sadly, is not out of her situation. She recently left her family and stayed with a friend for a few days. In the end, though, she returned home. With no immediate prospects for income and no savings, combined with the increasingly high cost of rent in her area, she feels she has no choice. Currently, she is training in a new job so that she can save money and then get out on her own, although the caregiving she still provides for her parents takes its toll on her body and her work schedule. She's hoping to be out soon, though. Maybe by Christmas. Of course, when she agreed to move in with her family to provide the care in the first place, she never anticipated things would be quite like they are.

And that's the rub. We never expect those closest to us to betray us in the way that narcissists do, but they do. As Christina says:

> Hindsight is 20/20, and narcissists are always waiting to get screwed, so they preemptively screw-- or maybe that's just paranoid people. But yeah, the rest of us loving, trusting people just assume that others will do unto us as we would, right? But the world is full of terrible people, like fathers and spouses-- the people who are supposed to support you at LEAST emotionally. How do we come back from that? I mean, we do, in our way, but it's a miracle.

A miracle, yes. One that all survivors of narcissistic abuse can hope to experience.

Beginnings

"I am one who loved not wisely but too well."

Shakespeare, *Othello*

PROGRAMMED

by Ayesha Fayyaz

They programmed me to become someone I never wanted to be
Someone unidentifiable
Someone invisible
Someone swollen with black soot of hope
Someone so sensitive, so reactive
Someone wandering-
Wandering in long corridors of past.

TRANSITIONS

by Meaghan Andrews

An obsession with grass and vines of honeysuckle
that twist and knot up the trunks of trees and limbs of azalea bushes.
Floral scents melding together in the air
to fight against the memory of a green Saturn, left caddy wampus
in a field of asphalt at two a.m. on a Thursday night.
A red neon light
        24/7 Ink
on my face.
Too late for a school night;
too late to learn how to add and subtract
using the loose change on your dresser.

THE FIRST PANCAKE

by Kristen Polito

This past Mother's Day, I rode my bicycle two cities over, slicing through humidity and foreboding; both of which felt so thick and heavy that I may as well have been treading water. Despite this, I was resolved to reach my destination and pay my dues. I was headed to my mother's house to visit with her and three of my four brothers. The calendar told me that I should.

Bear was in from Gainesville, Florida where he's recently begun medical school at the University of Florida. Bear will be the second of my mother's children to become a doctor. He is her third-born child.

My brother Paul, is already a practicing pediatrician living in Kansas City, Missouri with his wife and children. Paul is her second-born child and the first of my mother's children to become a doctor. As far as birth order is concerned, I am the first of my mother's children, but I am not a doctor, third, fourth, or fifth. Do you see the problem here? And not only am I her first-born, but I am her only girl. Do you feel the tension building?

From an anthropological standpoint, one might argue that there is this societal responsibility of dream fulfillment; one that exists in order to make a certain type of mother proud, satisfied. And by that theory, it's a daughter's obligation, whether she chooses to accept it or not.

Looking through my baby books, my mother's devotion to me is clearly evident. Milestones and other details are painstakingly recorded and my pictures are neatly arranged. When I reached school age, there was an endless supply of workbooks, reading material, and study guides to supplement my standard curriculum. She even advocated I.Q. testing for my admission to the Gifted and Talented program. However, the focus on academia was less gentle encouragement and more a mild form of fascism that created a state of perpetual anxiety that remains with me today.

My mother was a champion of guiding me through beauty pageants, local playhouse theater, movie or television casting auditions. My mother was equal parts Tiger Mom and Stage Mom, with a straight-forward manner and an eye so discerning that there was no doubt in my mind I possessed the capability to disappoint her. My mother and I maintained this ridiculous cliché up until I became very ill with my first major bout of anorexia, and by then, the only approval I was interested in was that of the voice in my head telling me to reach a new goal weight.

Because I *was* so blinded by naivety and desperation for her praise and acceptance during my formative childhood years, I'd failed to understand what was at stake. By focusing solely on achieving the dreams my mother had hand-picked for me, I hadn't considered establishing any of my own.

I realized these things at the age of 33.

Bear, who'd been in the living room with my mother and two youngest brothers, walked in just then. "I think I might be having an existential crisis," I said to him.

"I'm making pancakes," he announced, as if he hadn't heard me. He deftly moved through the kitchen, sorted and mixed the ingredients, finally setting the pan on the range.

Bear poured a small amount of batter in the pan and waited a few minutes. He carefully flipped the pancake over, and then, a minute later, slid it onto a paper plate and handed it to me. "Here", he said, "bring that outside and give it to Trixie" referring to his yellow lab, who'd been pacing the screened-in pool area, but, anticipating a treat, was now standing at attention by the French doors.

"What's wrong with this one?" I asked. "Don't you want it?"

"No, goof, that one's all messed up, see? It's, like, simultaneously burned *and* raw. It's the test pancake; you make a test pancake to see if you've got the pan at the perfect temperature yet. Everybody knows you throw out the first pancake."

He shoved the plate at me. "*Go on*, you're torturing Trixie."

I carried the plate out to the patio, walking slowly. Trixie smiled her doggie smile at me. I sat down on a deck chair with the plate in my lap, looking down at the pancake. It *was* burned. With my bare hands, I ripped the pancake in half. A little raw batter oozed out as I handed it over to Trixie's gaping maw. She gobbled the first half in seconds.

Then, without even thinking about it, I folded up the second half as small as I could make it and crammed the entire thing into my mouth. I allowed myself to acknowledge that I was burned and raw too, but no throw-away pancake. I suddenly felt ready to tell my mom I'll never be a doctor, but I've got my own dream now; and it's to be a writer.

I moved the huge mass of burned yet raw bread into the pouch of my right cheek, like a chipmunk. Chewing vigorously, I headed back into the house, my beauty pageant walk *on point.*

MOTHER AND DAUGHTER

by Meaghan Andrews

White rice yellowed with butter,
a black pattern of pepper protectively
 adhering to cooked grain--
breakfast, lunch, and dinner;
a spoonful of off-brand chocolate
frosting for dessert. A shared
single bedroom for me, you,
and your lovers. The familiar
burn of alcohol forever found
on your breath, but never
any money for meat.

MOTHER AND DAUGHTER was originally published in the Forage Poetry Journal.

PAINTING GOURDS

by Meaghan Andrews

A bench on a slope,
a bag full of orange, green, and yellow gourds.
Bruises of black,
blue edges fading into green on your face and around
scratches on your arms.
A gentle breeze to contrast with the chair you used
like a lion tamer
to hold back your husband the night before.
The breaking of glass,
the red and blue lights that were too late to save you
 from having to crawl through
the broken glass of a window or from the wine that had
replaced your husband's blood.

FINGERTIPS

by Kelly Baker

I don't want
the light to hit the water
because sleeping with you
leaves a bad taste in my mouth
and only when you beg
will I want to keep you going
and only when you close your eyes,
will I strike.
When the drapes close
and the stars come out from hiding,
I can still see you.

I can see in the dark.

You wouldn't believe what I can see in the dark.

Touch me how you like,
kiss me the way you feel.
I know so much,
from just the chills of your fingertips.

ALONE

by Jolene Hughes

I wait to relax until he is finally asleep, our bodies entwined, our breathing still labored. The sticky, heavy fragrance of sweat and sex clings to the air and the steam clouding the windows above our bed. The ripe moon's glow is muted by the moisture-slicked glass. No more words, moans, or creaking bed. We are done. My body betrayed me as my mind escaped, performing to meet expectations. Sex to take the edge off the stress of our troubled relationship. Sex to take a break from the spinning thoughts, the affairs, the alcohol-fueled rages that lose momentum when night's darkness yields to daybreak. Sex to prove how happy I am with him so he doesn't leave me and take the children where I can't protect them. From him.

I feel my soul disengage, disentangle from my body and his and turn away. The room becomes colder despite the heat radiating from our bodies. My soul withdraws from him in self-protection, defiance, subversively shifting allegiance from us to me. Soul-me rolls over, and it feels like when my unborn babies turned in my womb shortly before birth: a great shift that heaves my insides around. She pulls my most vulnerable self as she goes, that part locked away behind walls upon walls. She is so gentle to me as she curls around my scarred heart, her back facing the physical post-coital snare of limbs. It is as far from him as I dare to flee.

I am open and raw and exposed in this moment. It is too honest, and it is unsafe. Tomorrow I will smile and be nice. Maybe he will, too. We will kiss and pretend all is well in front of the children and his family and our friends and each other and he will count and take credit for our orgasms as usual. Nothing will change; the dance continues. But in this moment, I am aware and connected with the part of myself locked away behind those walls, protected from him and me by my soul, and I feel it all.

It is dark in here without the moonlight. I hope he doesn't feel my tears on his chest.

WHAT DOESN'T KILL YOU

by Kate Davis

"What doesn't kill you makes you stronger..."
I think that saying
Is wrong.
Maybe.
Physically,
I was traumatized.
The emotional upheaval,
I am sure,
Could have killed me.
If I had been elderly,
Or had a pre-existing condition--
Cardiovascular disease--
I would have broken
My broken heart.
Stronger?
I don't know.
I may die
a few years earlier--
After surviving my Cataclysmic,
Heart wrenching,
Rejection and loss.
Instead I fight,
And grow stronger.
Maybe.

JAMES

by Meaghan Andrews

A name found in Kenny's Key West in New Orleans belonging to a furious storm of

alcohol,
car racing,
sexual desire,
and discipline.

The green Saturn he raced--crashed;
the sexual desire evicted me from my mother's bedroom, the only one in our apartment--
displaced me to a floral couch where occasionally he would find me half-empty beer in hand.
Alcohol broke my mother's nose and left them both passed out by 5pm so they could
get back up at midnight and take me to dark parking lots lit only by green burning neon lights.
Discipline, a skill he tried to depart on me with kitchen timers and a leather belt. Each bruise
a trophy, a fading black and blue realization of my life.

JAMES was originally published in the Bitchin' Kitsch.

SO MUCH TO SEE, 1957

by Jeanie Greensfelder

I followed him up three flights of stairs.
An inventor, he pressed three buttons by his door,
made it buzz ajar, and said *Open Sesame.*

I saw orange canvas butterfly chairs,
cushions on a low foam pad,
and a matted jute rug.

Bookcases stood along burlap walls
and egg crates covered the ceiling.
I stared at a self-portrait of his wife,

an artist with a black braid on one shoulder.
Twenty years of trouble, he said.
She's leaving.

Steered into his darkroom,
he shined magic yellow lights
and turned paper into photographs.

In his shop he assembled parts,
making the lamp he'd offered
for my college dorm room.

I saw so much when I was there,
but failed to see this would be
my future home.

A version of this poem was published in *Biting the Apple*, Pencilled In, 2012

FORMALDEHYDE

by Bella Lord

I let you dissect me in your funeral home
And the operation table felt like a throne
The mortician has treated this body well
Though my neck will bruise and my feet will swell
Your bedsheets are far too heavy to lift
I mention your mother and your eyes shut stiff
What am I doing here, so late at night?
What is that hurting those deep brown eyes?
Everyone loves you, a brilliant find
I'll give you my soul for a piece of your mind
But that's not enough for you, you have a fix
And mine is falling for your poisoned tricks
I know you have a complex, of some kind
threads stitching your heart will soon unwind
You roughed up my corpse and dressed up your doll
But I smile, because, I'm the belle of the ball
It feels like I haven't seen you for months
It feels like you ate
My soul
For lunch
You insist you love the green in my eyes
But your lashes are always longer than mine
I get it, your mother put you through hell
But I'm
not her
And you're not well
Over your bed hangs a funeral pall
But I'd rather be an object than nothing at all
You love the attention, I've so much to give!
Never mind how long I've yet to live
"you're all mine" you gently sighed
Your lips inject me with formaldehyde

SAVAGE MOTHER

by Catherine Wald

Mahakali

Accessorized with limbs, skulls

Demon devourer

Mangler of evil

Long-tongued leacher of toxins

Darkest Durga, harbinger of purge

Unquenchable avenger

My pulsing jugular awaits your sword.

STAGE MOM

by Kristen Polito

I was raised the only daughter of one *very* ambitious stage mom. There, I said it.

In just a few short years, she deftly facilitated all that was necessary to make manifest the basic building blocks of an anxious childhood: beauty pageants, head-shots, talent agencies, auditions, the whole shebang.

My mother was hellbent that I attain *success!* so she encouraged me, coached me, and cajoled me She permed and curled my flat and lifeless mouse-brown hair. She dolled-me up, slapped on the paint; she inventoried and camouflaged my endless flaws.

She forfeited her own personal time for the sake of my theoretical triumph. There was, supposedly, some favorable outcome on the horizon. She was in the business of creating opportunities and, if there was an opportunity to be had, I'd better damn well seize it.

My mother, the consummate momager, not only showcased me in beauty pageants but also had me enrolled as a client in a modeling & talent agency. I had a professional resume and headshots. She'd take me on "go- see's" to various auditions with strict instructions to be effusive and charismatic.

I, both wanting to please her and also wanting to be a STAR! (*hello, I was a little girl, ya know*), went right along with it, excited at first, then quickly resigned to feigning enthusiasm for that which I began to tire of. The whole concept and everything it demanded of me forced me beyond my introverted comfort zone, into another dimension entirely.I was naturally shy, and terribly insecure. This only exacerbated it. It made me anxious; and it made me chronically depressed.

Throughout my short stint on the "Pageant Circuit" and as a client of "various talent agencies" being sent out to television and movie auditions, my mother would falsify my weight and measurements on both my composite card and my resume to appear more appealing as a candidate for potential work.

Result: My mother instilled a fixation with the number on the scale, a number which, at that age, and at that point in my development, would have been quite arbitrary. I learned that ladies are ashamed about their weight, that they lie about their weight, and that what they actually are born with is not right, totally unacceptable.

Around age eight, I had already failed at the other "girl-stuff"too: I was a klutz. The ballet, tap, modern, jazz dance classes were wasted on my bumbling nature. It did not help me become more graceful or poised. Additionally, gymnastics was an epic failure. I was a giant amongst tiny, perfect elves, much too large for the sport. I was way more WNBA than USAG.

But in her defense, my mom was young and inexperienced. After all, I was her first-born. I was her only girl, too. Her shining star, as my aunt would later tell me. Her one shot at whatever dreams she wanted through that of a female child. I'd been a pretty, bright, expressive girl with a nearly eidetic memory for scripts. So her enthusiasm was both understandable and simultaneously condemnable when it finally began to wane in middle school when I became chubby and awkward.

But I don't blame her. I really don't. I don't really attribute my eating disorder to anything she or my dad said or did. Family of origin is only one small piece of the eating disorder puzzle. Plus, nobody knew any better.

Nowadays, we have positive body image campaigns, an effort to educate the public about eating disorders, advocacy, what have you. It could all stand to be improved, revamped, made more widely available, but at least, it's getting there.

And while body image is finally being discussed in mainstream media channels, it still remains a taboo subject in a great many households. To be honest, I'm flabbergasted that this could still be the case, as the issue of body image affects almost everyone in today's highly visual-centric society.

When I was growing up, there was none of the media coverage. No "Real Beauty" campaigns. The Surgeon General didn't even publicly address mental illness until I was a junior in high school. Mental illness bore a terrible stigma, even worse than it does today, so no one was even comfortable having those kind of family conversations. My mother didn't know any better and was possibly mimicking even more arcane notions than these.

Don't get me wrong, it's not as if my mom would have a legitimately open dialogue around that topic now. Presently, this is still very much the parent-child dynamic in our relationship. Stilted, difficult conversations on perpetually uncomfortable topics. We never talk just to "chat" like I imagine other mothers and daughters doing.

Despite having been dangerously ill from anorexia several times, there's no surviving part of the "adult me" that doesn't feel as though I'm "too much" in the presence of my mother. I'm far "too emotional, too volatile, too selfish, too extreme, too intense, too indulgent, too, too much."

Read: "Unacceptable" which probably means "too large" which would definitely mean "too fat." Better change that number on the scale. Or at least, the number on the paper.

No one can find out how wrong I am.

PAUL

by J. Kathleen Marcus

My tenth grade English teacher walked over to me during class, stroked my long hair, brought some of it to his face, and inhaled deeply. In front of everyone. And then he gave me a wink. The wink was to let me know we had a secret. It was the first of many.

I had smoked a joint before class and my hair reeked of it, but the fifty-four-year-old me looks back on the moment with horror. And also with a deep understanding that this forty-something-year-old man had just given a fifteen-year-old girl a moment of intimacy that made her feel special and opened her up wide to the liberties that men would take in the name of love.

Two years later when Paul discovered I had mailed my college application essays, he demanded to see my copies. I gave him the sad mess of carbons – it was 1980. And then he ripped the pages to shreds, forcefully throwing the bits of paper in my face. I hadn't asked him for help. I hadn't discussed the essays with him. I hadn't even asked that he proofread them in those days before spellcheck. I hadn't written about him. But I was taking a step toward escaping our relationship, and he hated me for it.

As he brutally dissected my essays (with their many typos), he yelled. *How did I think I was able to write well without his help? Why had I been so stupid? Bennington was a long shot for me. Had I forgotten who I was? Had I forgotten I had no education of any consequence?* I was crying quietly as he did to my confidence what he had done to my essays – tearing it into pieces and throwing it in my face. I was humiliated. He was right, I knew. I had blown what little chance I had to go to Bennington. I would never manage without him. And now, when he finally went silent, I would feel his anger and disapproval wash over me until he moved this incident into the always-available file of my affronts to him. Everything I had ever done that angered or displeased him lived forever, ready to be used as ammunition against me the next time I failed him. There would always be a next time.

Paul was considered an odd teacher but an easy A and my registration in his class had been arbitrary. It was just another section of tenth grade English. Paul had student pets, one of whom I knew and who encouraged me to come to meetings of the school literary magazine which Paul ran. I found myself in his presence more and more. He noticed me, plucking me from the mass of working class kids smoking in the stairwells of a suburban high school near New York City.

Eventually, Paul would beat me, rape me, trap me in his bedroom, and push me down the stairs, but my mind still goes back to the day he smelled my hair. He was a big man, physically much like his idol Ernest Hemingway. Imposing and frightening with beefy arms that he always used to punctuate his sentences, he had a big. warm laugh that could envelop you. When he smelled my hair, he had let me know we had a secret and having a secret meant I was special. As a poor kid with holes in her shoes and a long history of homelessness and foster care, there was nothing I needed more than to be special.

It wasn't long after I became one of his special students that I was invited to an evening at his house to listen to jazz and talk about poetry while drinking beer. That is what his student pets got to do. I was fifteen years old. These evenings were secrets, of course. None of us were old enough to drink. More secrets. Secrets made me special. More secrets made me more special.

He told me I was brilliant, mature, strong, such a survivor. When he invited me to stay in his guest room one night after jazz/poetry/beer, I felt it was one step closer to be in his family, to be the most special. I hadn't yet learned the signs I would know so well when he had passed into his drunkenness without rules. When he tapped on the door and opened it standing naked in the doorway, I went numb. He wanted to let me know I was welcome to join him in his room down the hall. I don't remember if I said anything or shook my head, but I curled up in his guest bed after he had left, shaking. I don't think I was particularly afraid. The feeling that washed over me was sadness. I wasn't special. He just wanted to sleep with me. This was life in my mother's house all over again. Strange men walking into my bedroom at night.

Paul knew I had grown up being sexually assaulted. He had made sympathetic sounds and told me I was amazing. And now he was standing naked at the door. Sadness became a sense of betrayal and blossomed into fury. *He knew! He fucking knew how I had been hurt and he was ready to do it to me. He was the same as all the other men my mother brought into our twisted world.*

Finally I wrote a speech in my head and marched over to his bedroom. *How dare you? I thought you were different! You know I grew up with this. How can you be so insensitive*? In my mind I was asserting myself. I was taking control. I was being mature. I wasn't the helpless little girl I had been in my mother's house. Paul started to cry, apologized profusely about "getting his signals crossed," and then he hugged me. A long time. Within six months, I lived in that house.

For three years I was his lover, surrogate parent to his two young sons, and lived in a clench ready to be berated for my failings. The toilet paper roll had been replaced upside down, when it had never occurred to me there was a right and wrong way for toilet paper to roll. The coffee mugs had to be preheated with hot water so the coffee didn't cool down upon meeting a cold container. His desperate disorganized life was never to be questioned. The day I organized his mountain of junk mail and unpaid bills, a show of love and adult responsibility on my part (in my head anyway), I thought he would kill me. Within the first year I began to stutter, never having stuttered in my life. We were inseparable, except for Friday nights when he went to Nolan's bar. I would lie in bed waiting for the sound of his car in the driveway and wondering how bad it would be this time. Every once in a while, I still think I hear his car.

I knew at the time that what I really wanted was for Paul to be the parent I so desperately needed. I told no one. It was a childish fantasy of which I was ashamed. Only years later did I realize that Paul did become a parent. He became my mother who gave and withdrew approval with no warning, lashed out with hateful fury when I least expected it, and who disappeared into drugs and alcohol to some place beyond my reach.

To the amazement of both Paul and me, that shredded college application led to acceptance, a scholarship, and escape. When I first arrived at college, having put what I could into a duffel bag and taken a Greyhound from Port Authority, I felt an immobilizing ache. I missed him. But as the days passed without hearing his voice, I opened myself to other voices. By the end of my first semester, I had aborted a pregnancy Paul thought was his but wasn't. And in my second semester, once I had managed to carry or ship all that I owned (mostly books) to my dorm, I broke up with him. I have no memory of how. I remember the tightness in my chest, the terror he would drive up to Vermont and do...I didn't know what. I had left his world and feared he would do something to destroy my new one. But he didn't. Within a fairly short time he had a new girlfriend. He told me all the ways she was wonderful – an adult with a job and a more independent life. Each description of her was an intended criticism of me but all I felt was relief. He couldn't hurt me anymore. I was free.

Paul died twenty-five years later while making coffee in the kitchen of the Vermont cabin to which he had retired. Just clutched his chest and fell to the floor. I hadn't seen him since the summer before I went to law school and had no part in his life with a new woman and their child together. But I try to imagine the moment of his death. I have a mental picture, know all his meticulous breakfast preparations. I want to have seen it. To be sure. I want an actual picture of his death, but I will never know what his death was like. I will never have a sense of release, of revenge.

But of one thing I am certain. The coffee mugs had been warmed.

DUNGEONS

by Rehana Campbell

You stood at the sidelines watching me play,
Silently cheering me on.
You stood at the sidelines watching me fight,
Silently pushing her on.
You are such a dichotomy,
Staring at me blankly, a familiar bittersweet harmony.
Sad eyes mixed with bad lies,
I despise every second you betrayed me.
As my only source of reality the child in me knows bribery,
Those sad eyes are a part of me,
Ingenious in your treachery.
So withered and so tired,
Those eyes of yours endorsed abuse,
Told her truths, yet told no truth.
It was my heart so far apart from your cathartic start,
I am a being of true meaning,
While you're a slave to her dungeons of dark art.

THE PARENT-PLEASING TRAP

by Kristen Polito

My mom is first and foremost a pragmatist.

Straightforward and matter-of-fact, she doesn't typically let emotion distract her. I have to assume that these characteristics are innate, for this has been her nature as far back as I recall. Compounding that, it could certainly be argued that 14-plus years of raising severely autistic children has necessitated an intensified level of efficiency and practicality.

To the nth degree.

From my own perspective, these traits can sometimes seem remote or standoffish. If I am in a particularly emotionally raw state, her straightforward manner can feel critical and disapproving. I need to emphasize that this is how I experience our relationship, and may or may not be accurate.

My relationship with my mom is complicated and confusing. Landmines, just under the surface of our 33-year connection, threaten to erupt at every interaction. I am her first-born. And her only girl.

Naturally, there is the implication that dreams in the realm of "feminine" glory or success are my responsibility to fulfill. How could it not be intense? My mom wanted so much for me. She has done so much for me.

As her firstborn, she literally made me the center of her life from the very beginning. Looking through my baby books, her devotion is apparent; milestones and other details are painstakingly recorded in beautiful handwriting. Thousands of pictures are neatly labeled and arranged. She guided my educational path by teaching me to read as well as supplementing my classwork with workbooks, tutoring and other resources. During elementary school, she advocated I.Q. testing so that I had the opportunity to enter the gifted and talented program.

I became, and continue to be, an avid reader and capable writer as a result of my mom's influence.

She encouraged and supported me in the undertaking of any extracurricular activity in which I demonstrated an interest.

She taught me morals and ethics. She read me the Bible and brought me to church.

Through the years, she created homemade Halloween costumes of professional quality and indulged my childish whims.

Together we drew, completed projects, took walks and baked cookies.

My mom is a really amazing person. A really good mom. However, as a highly emotional, rapid-cycling bipolar, eating disordered adult-child, I struggle with a lot of internal, self-imposed pressure in relation to our dynamic. Regardless of how objectively successful or unsuccessful I happen to be, I have always felt as though I haven't pleased her. Fallen short of the mark. Without exception.

The underlying concern that I am "not good enough" isn't a recent sentiment. I didn't begin feeling this way during my recent and significant struggles with physical and mental health. It didn't start when my marriage dissolved, I claimed bankruptcy, lost my job, and fell into legal trouble. It's not a neurosis stemming from angst-riddled teenage years or even from middle-school.

This desperate desire to "perfectly please" my Mom has been with me always. I remember the anxiety in elementary school, in preschool even. I probably was a stressed-out, high-strung baby.

One particularly traumatic memory from 3rd grade demonstrates both the longevity and irrationality which characterize my fears.

My teacher, Ms. F., had administered a pop-quiz in which students were to complete sentences utilizing appropriate punctuation. Apparently, the teacher was having a bit of an off-day because her reaction to the less-than-stellar performance of the class was over-kill. In a loud and (what I remember to be) intimidating voice designed to humiliate, she listed the students names who had failed to use periods at the end of their sentences and would, therefore, be receiving an F grade. I remembered being terrified to go home that day, dreading the inevitable confrontation in which I would have to present my mother with such a shameful abomination of school-work.

I suppose this was my first experience with failure, and I was unprepared to handle it. Ridiculous as it sounds, that experience shook me to the core. The terror in potentially disappointing my mom was sufficient to remain in my memory to this day.

From that moment on, my subconscious had become altered. My preexisting anxiety to please became augmented by the new knowledge that I possessed the capability to disappoint. The sheer inevitability of it was overwhelming.

I felt as though I was defective, somehow.

At age 33, there's a part of me that remains overly reliant on her for validation and approval. This is an entirely different type of acknowledgment than that of which I seek from the ever-evolving relationship with my father. With my mom I feel childish and stunted, as though I'm still earning gold stars to stick onto one of those achievement poster boards lining the sad, fluorescent hallways of anyschool, anytown, USA.

I am the first to admit that, given my genetic predispositions (bipolar I, anxiety and borderline personality disorder diagnoses), I experience the parental dynamic at a higher intensity than others. However, I am not alone in the seemingly uphill battle that is parent-pleasing.

A very dear friend of over 20 years recently sent me a message containing this excerpt:

> So my dad was here for the week. He asked about you and we were reminiscing about that trip to the Keys. He loved telling everyone that he would wake up before dawn to go out and monitor your runs. I think I joined you once and then just kept sleeping the other times. Haha. And that wretched barracuda encounter while snorkeling. He is so fond of you and really wishes you well. Isn't the father-daughter dynamic so strange...I am still constantly trying to impress him and win his approval even at this age. (Husband's name) teases me about it. I tell him to remember this for his own two daughters – he needs to give them constant praise and approval.

This, to me, demonstrates that no one's relationship with their parents is perfect. No one is exempt from the desire for parental approval... and (sometimes) the feeling that it's just out of reach.

The truth is, I haven't failed my mom. Not at all. Even at my rock- bottom, my mom has loved and supported me unconditionally. Yes, she may scowl, speak sharply or give me the silent treatment. But it's less about whether I have achieved that all-so-elusive state of "success" (whatever that is) and more about her wanting "more" for me. No matter what, she wants more. More for me. And more for my brothers.

Because she loves us, she wants more. More than anything.

WITH MONSTER

by Amy Oestreicher

With Monster, I imagine myself like little Red Riding Hood who strayed from the path because a seemingly friendly wolf tricked her into it. The flowers off the side of the road were just too pretty. But that's the thing – the flower farthest from the path is always the prettiest one. Straying from the path led to danger and being victimized by the wolf – so now she has a skewed vision of what is safe and what isn't. She lost trust for those things in the world. A beautiful flower was not a beautiful flower anymore – it was a device that a manipulative wolf used to lead her astray. Not even the flowers were friends. She became numb.

Now you are Red Riding Hood walking the same path but the wolf is gone. The trees keep rustling so you think he is out there ready to pounce on you, but really you are safe in the outside world and that rustling is just a squirrel gathering acorns. So what you have to do is put yourself in the NOW, see that tail of the squirrel, and recognize that nothing is out to get you anymore.

I was so happy Monster got to see my family when he drove me home from Mohonk Mountain and mom had invited him to dinner. I was so happy he got to see our family bicker like we usually do and laugh over stupid stuff. And I was so disappointed when he told me later, "Your house is like the far off fantasyland of the boys who never want to grow up." My first reaction was, "*Are you kidding?*" But his blabber was so convincing that by the end I bought it because it made sense, and so I got mad at my family, even though I think I was really mad at him for taking away the magic I saw in my family. But all that energy got stuck in translation, and so it just got misdirected at my family and myself. I just hated the world, everyone and everything in it except Monster, whom I hated the most but clung to shamelessly in disgust because that was all I had. I hated myself for that.

That small, safe world was just enough for me – happy Thanksgivings, going from audition to audition, fun little sibling arguments, if there is one word to describe our family and the life that I had it was 'loud.' Loud and bright. Now it feels quiet and dark and very detached from the real world. I stay numb now to not think about everything I've lost. Maybe

I need to face the emptiness of my world and accept it in order to fill it back up again. The landscape is dark and bleak. But I miss the world I used to have – a magical world where everything was magic and I was just fascinated by everything. I was alive. I miss my family. I miss the six of us on vacation. I miss the safety I would find in wrapping my arms around my brothers as we walked down the city streets.

I remember the first time Monster and I went to a show together, and I was still in awe of him. We were walking behind this woman pushing a stroller really slowly. Monster had hypnotized me so much into thinking he only had godlike intentions, that I just assumed he was going to comment on the beauty of the woman's step, like making some deep, insightful comment about the high truths of how she carried herself, which is what I thought he did. I thought he looked at everything from this inspired, esoteric perspective – he was superhuman. He didn't get annoyed at anything. So I widened my big blue sparkly eyes and tried to do my best Monster impression and find something beautiful and wise about that moment so I'd have something to say when he shed his own enlightenment.

But he just ended up saying, "god, some people are so slow. They have nerve taking up the whole street like that."

The more I got to know him, the more I discovered how self-righteous and indignant he really was. His insecurity made me insecure about myself since I based my whole world on his shoulders. When I had really uncovered the jackass he was, so much that I myself had landed way down past rock-bottom and didn't care about anything anymore, we were in a cab together and he didn't like the way the cab driver was taking us. He completely lost his temper and starting cursing the poor guy out – *fuck you and fuck this and fuck you're an asshole you fuck, fuck, fuck* – to the point where I was really embarrassed to be with Monster in the car. What a grumpy angry old man. And the poor driver was apologizing for whatever just to shut him up. It was so awkward, and it made me hate my world, just wishing I had a video camera so I could show this to someone so they could understand this whole crazy situation. When you don't have an outside perspective, it feels completely surreal.

Since I aspired to be like him, the grumpier, angrier, and uglier he got, the more I became that way. Almost out of resentment, like spiting myself for being so foolish, blowing all my marbles on this one person who I deemed the ultimate beauty of the world. That's what I get for being so stupid. I am so angry at him. What an asshole. I feel like, okay, I've caught it; I've caught the angry bug. How do I get it out of me now that I know there are healthier and more effective ways to deal with it? I want a boyfriend, I want my freedom back, and I want back the things I've lost.

For some reason, I totally surrendered myself to Monster. I gave up everything I had and presented it before him, like on Yom Kippur when you lay all your sins and secrets at God's feet. I just became a movie camera filming videos for him to watch every lesson. My heart became an open door. I thought I was being deeply spiritual in surrendering everything I had to him, but really I was making a deal with the devil because he took it and fed upon it, like a hungry lion mastering its prey's smell so he can attack.

And so, therefore, I lost my sense of trust as well. I lost my willingness to so freely surrender. I lost my faith in God because Monster was my embodiment of Him. The world became spiritless, directionless, and empty like a big black hole. I thought by being completely honest with him I was confiding in a fellow truth seeker, but I was just giving a robber my home address, my credit card number, my house keys, and what hours to find me. How could anything be safe anymore? I lost my sense of safety in the outside world – I didn't know who I could lean on. I thought Monster was my everything. I didn't know what my family was now. And I felt no safety in *myself* – here I had relied on myself as my own anchor in the wide open sea – I thought I was an adult, I thought I could handle this. I thought he was holy. I remember spreading tofu cream cheese on a bagel in our apartment while mom questioned me about staying over at Monster's until 3 in the morning and I started yelling and crying saying *no it's fine!* At that point I was starting to get a clue that he was crossing boundaries but it didn't seem threatening, it felt exciting even though I didn't know what was coming next, so I just wanted mom to stay the hell out of it – I knew what I was doing, right?

I know I can't blame myself for trying to make those decisions myself because when I look at this all with perspective, I know I was young and innocent and found this all to be terribly exciting at first – imagine this:

You are really religious and worship God so faithfully, and one day he actually appears! You thought he was only a metaphor! But no, he appears sitting on a tree branch, not only that, but he takes your hand and invites you up to his special VIP cloud kingdom! Everyone is telling you that you're crazy, it's a mistake, but they don't understand. Only you do because you are just that spiritual, and they could never know! You take his hand in the middle of the night – you climb out of your bedroom window and make a grand escape so nobody can catch you – and you ascend to the higher things. But surprisingly, he takes you down into the center of the earth, and you start to feel the heat, the fire building up, making you sweat. He takes off his long white robe and you discover that he is really the devil in disguise. You feel the fires of hell surrounding you, and there is no way out; you'll get burned. You freeze yourself in an ice cube to stay alive, because only heathens can stand this kind of heat.

And then you find out that heaven doesn't really exist; it's really just this dirty, sweaty, hot place. All the demons in the underworld surround you and point their long, crooked fingers at you, laughing all the way to the bank. And the shame is just too much. That ice cube keeps you nice and cold so you don't have to feel the heat of that shame. How silly you were, Red Riding Hood. How silly you were. How deeply you trusted. Those wide blue sparkling innocent eyes.

I miss living life with a tape recorder in my head so I could explain it all so poetic and insightfully to Monster every Friday. When someone asked Arthur Miller once if he was working on any new play now, he responded, I don't know. I might be. And I think that epitomizes how I feel – as artists, we are always on the lookout for new inspiration. We are always creating art in our heads. Any little speck of a moment might explode into this mighty mountainous idea for a play, story, song, anything. And that is what makes living an adventure. My problem in my innocence was that I made Monster my art.

Did a perfectly innocent life have to be blasted apart? Does what go up really have to come down? Can't it just float there for a while?

He didn't steal my soul-juice, I know that that is always within me, just frozen, but – I don't know. I'm grieving too much to be poetic here. I want a good cry. I want to clutch my teddy bear and long for the days of yore. I hate facing all of that because it makes me feel empty inside.

But cheer up, Red Riding Hood. You have lost, but you are working so hard to gain now. Gaining in every way from every angle. You take to god like a bad habit – he fooled you once and he'll fool you again and again, but that's just life: you fall down and you get back up but from a different place and into new uncharted territory, a new path. Just gotta laugh it off, dust yourself off, and start all over again.

This essay was inspired by an excerpt from Amy's book (My Beautiful Detour), her TEDx talk on being a "Detourist," and one of Amy's full length original dramas, Flicker and a Firestarter, currently in development.

MY ISSUES WITH LOVE, FUCK!

by Rehana Campbell

Sometimes I notice that I don't know how to love.
It's so prevalent,
it sticks to me like the summer air.
I have so much to give,
yet it stands as a frozen brick in my heart.
It is not cold, however.
It's frozen in time.
It is me and I'm young,
quite small really.
I can feel the openness I've left behind,
so electric some even stayed with me.

Now I am here,
the sweetness of love has sprinkled my lips,
yet I feel his earthiness as warm and repulsive.
What things have I not unearthed within myself to feel such repulsion of
such a beauty?
Or is it a matter of instinct?
Tell me why I must feel such conflictions!
Ah... but I know, the answer is simple.
I was raised by a love that was ever so conditioned.

Lost in the Middle

"Though this be madness, yet there is method in't."

Shakespeare, *Hamlet*

THAT THING YOU SAID THAT ONE NIGHT

by Molly Pennington

"I'm marrying you."

Brian held my face in his hands while he said it. I pulled away--his grip tightened. Hot on my cheeks. He grasped me in that way that's supposed to be romantic. So you can get taken. Like when your lover, in his poet blouse, Fabio-hair grazing your décolletage, overwhelms with you with zealous kisses that inflame your core. Yeah. It wasn't like that.

It was like being buried in sand. At three in the morning. And choosing sleep instead of exit. *Just go. Just leave*. That voice in your head that gets smaller, not louder, every time you think it. I recognized the nudge. That fish of me, wiggling. My essence in quicksand somewhere deep.

I never listened to my gut back then. It would take decades before I learned that language.

He said it again: "I am marrying you." It wasn't a proposal.

I squirmed. He pulled my head back to meet his eyes. I sank. I couldn't marry him. Cellie would kill me. She had already nursed me through at least five Brian Break-ups. *Cellie*?

Brian must have seen my pause. My fade. Because he countered with an irresistible doozy: "It's going to be different this time. Do you hear me?" He said it urgent. "I am never going to hurt you again."

I'm never going to hurt you again.

That *hooked* me. I would repeat that line, that moment, for years. He's not going to hurt me. I'm never going to be hurt again. I thought it meant love because I thought love meant relief. No more fighting. No break-ups. No tears. Bruises. Insults. Slights or slurs. No abuses. I neglected to think of what I would get. In my mind, it was only about what would cease.

A few months later, I stood on the edge of a cliff, with Cellie, my maid-of-honor, by my side. And I married him.

I should have known better. You know I should have known better.

My little fish was a-wiggle, nauseous, and turning. I pushed down the tickle. I was the most passively reckless sky-diver on the planet. I jumped off that cliff knowing full well that there wasn't a parachute, or a safety net, or some air mattress filled with money. I knew it was just stalagmites. An impaling. I kinda didn't care. I was already so worn down by then.

Just do what he says. Stay out of his way.

I can't blame him after all. He was already damaged in that way where his soul leaked out and evaporated. Like a puddle on a hot day. I mean, that was before I came along. Some personality disorder, narcissism, borderline, whatever. He later refused all therapists once he realized that sessions wouldn't mean he could gang up on me with the help of an expert.

I get why he liked me, though early on I didn't. I was inquisitive and poetic, but desperate. Cheerful and optimistic, but so fucking insecure. I was pretty, but I had no idea. I was built like a pin-up, but I felt totally fat. And I wanted love the way that a baby wants its bottle or a shark wants blood. I was a child and an addict for love.

He was the prom king at my high school back when I ran with a group known as "The Sisters of Doom." Because we lined our eyes in dark kohl. I had a thick mane of jet hair that I despised because it wouldn't take a perm. I listened to The Smiths and wore a black leather jacket. I pulled charcoal tights over my legs most days. Didn't speak unless spoken too. I was bent on hiding my "wrong side of the tracks" pedigree with clouds and mystique.

When I ran into Brian up at college, in the cafeteria, he said "hey!" And he lifted his chin. I mistook this tepid acknowledgement for some kind of grace. He had golden curls that hung around his nape. A surfer's glow. He used to run around campus shirtless, torso oiled with sunscreen. Later, back in our home town, I caught him staring at me. I didn't recognize it as a proprietary gaze. An interest that sought control. I thought it meant that I was lucky, finally notable. He asked me out.

On our first date he threw needles.

"Your legs are so white!"

"You're the least athletic person I've ever seen."

"You don't know anything about politics."

"You're way too bold with your opinion."

"I'm not drinking too much. That's an insult!"

"You're not very courteous, are you?"

I was 21. I hadn't figured out how to live quietly yet--lord, I was trying. I would end up not being that great at strangling my fish. Eventually, I would save it.

Brian acted like he didn't like me the whole time we were out that first night. At one point he started to upbraid a pizza guy. And then he curled up, knees to chest, by some tree outside and claimed the whole world hated him.

I kneeled. I took his hand. I was careful. To not make him think that he was weak or weird or something. I liked weird.

"No one hates you."

"They do," he pouted.

"I don't," I smiled. Then he tore his hand away. So that was that.

But then he called. He wanted to go out again. And again. Cellie hated him. When he spoke, she rolled her eyes. He argued that he couldn't go to a gay bar because he didn't want to deal with all the attention.

"You won't get hit on. Trust me," said Cellie. She had a cigarette and a scowl. I kept Brian and Cellie apart after that. She had no qualms with calling him out. And he couldn't be questioned. Or he'd threaten to leave. I didn't want him to have to curl up.

So I gave him: care, concern, compliments, companionship. I don't know why I thought it my duty. He didn't say it. But there was this contract. This understanding. He was the prom king. And I would never be good enough. You know how it goes. Finally, after a rollercoaster summer, he broke up with me. He didn't love me after all. I remember his announcement. He was proud and assertive: I don't love you. At all.

Sorry. Bye.

I took the news as if the skin was removed off my forearms, revealing tiny sprouted cities made of humiliation and pain. After a few months I stopped pining. That's when I got the letter. A love letter. He drew a rainbow on it. The gist was that actually he did love me. He needed me to drop everything and fly to Maui where he was working as a tennis pro.

"But I just got over you," I said.

"But I love you. I love you. Now I know that."

So I left college, maxed a credit card and flew to Maui. And it was all sweetness, aloha, and pineapple. For the first few hours. My first mistake was that I didn't bring condoms. Then I left the bread out. I put the lid on the toothpaste wrong. I didn't do the crunches to flatten my abs. I wasn't courteous enough.

"How come you never use basic manners with me?" he yelled. Then he would storm out. And return with gifts.

I would tell him, gently, so gently, that I needed to move home. Finish college. He would rage. Then despair. I flew home for Christmas and I met someone else, this other guy. That made me a whore, but one who Brian still wanted, still needed. He sent me enormous flower arrangements ten days in a row. So I broke up with the other guy. Even though Cellie loved him. Even though I felt funny and smart when I was with him. Warm and easy. I didn't recognize love without tension. That other guy didn't plead when I ended it. I took that as indifference, not respect. His eyes teared, "I want you to be happy."

Brian came back from Maui. Angrier than ever. We moved in together. He started to push me and break things. It was my fault. For dating that other guy. For talking back. Why couldn't I just be courteous? I left six months later. I graduated. I moved to a big city. I got a job. Entered graduate school. And then a year later, I called Brian. Out of the wild blue.

Why would I do that? Why would I call him? Quit grad school? Get married. How could I be so stupid?

I used to think my reasons were complicated, a crazy quilt of dysfunction stitched across my youth. Actually, it could all be reduced to a few clichés: Absentee father. Molestation at 3. Date rape in high school. Love affair with a brutalist early in college (rape, battery, stalking, etcetera.).

After all that, and the thing that came next, the thing that made me call him, a promise from Brian, my onetime brute, was enough to slay me. Maybe we would erase the past? Start anew?

I didn't realize that I was in serious trouble until a few months into the marriage when Brian threatened to kill me. That's a lie. That's what he would say. I'm still not good at redress. At telling it like it is without going over every detail with skepticism. With Brian's own suspicions about my every move.

It started while we were registering for wedding gifts. Our registry was this huge beacon that we were not the type of people who should be getting married. Brian chose a single black towel sheet. One pewter goblet. Then he aimed the scanner at the most expensive television in the store.

"Please," I begged, "don't. People will think we expect it."

"So what," Brian laughed.

That wasn't the night we fought about it. That came months later. My mom was always the type to try and get my brother and me whatever we had "registered" for in life. Somehow, even when there wasn't any money, electric blue cowboy boots, Harley Davidson jackets, Ralph Lauren sweaters, and Guess jeans would appear under the tree.

I wasn't surprised that she wanted to give us that colossal television set. She asked if she could get us one that was the same size, but a different brand. A lot cheaper.

"No," Brian said, "It has to be the Sony."

My gut twisted up. My fishtail stuck in a curl.

My mom's face fell. It was the kind of money that made a difference.

That had always made a difference to us. But then she figured out a way to get the Sony. We'd have to buy it on her store credit card. Use a coupon.

We were in the car on the way to buy it, when I finally told Brian how I felt.

I was sitting in the passenger seat. And by this time, I was great at being careful.

"I don't want to buy this TV. My mom can't afford it."

Brian was silent.

"Can't we just get the other one? Please?"

He didn't say a word. That's why he'll say that I'm lying about him trying to kill me. Threatening to kill me? I guess we can downgrade it to trying to scare me.

Brian sped up, revving the engine as we tore down the street. He slammed the breaks as we hit a red light. I flew forward, yanked back by the seat belt.

"What are you doing?" I asked, flustered.

The light switched to green and Brian floored the pedal. He pulled tight to the car in front of us. I braced for impact. Then he swerved into to the next lane. The car swiveled. Recovered. He raced to the tail of the next car. I watched the gas needle move past sixty.

"Stop it," I screamed.

Then he revved to seventy, on a city street, weaving between cars. Ignoring my pleas. When he slammed the breaks again, I opened the door. Leapt out. I don't know what I expected. One of those apologies?

But he zoomed away. Left me there. I was exactly forty blocks from home. This was a problem. My purse was in the car. It was freezing out and I had a sprained foot. A few days earlier, I'd fallen down the stairs. My foot was a swollen eggplant. No cast. Just stay off of it, the E.R. doc told me. Then he offered me crutches. Brian wouldn't let me take them because of the extra cost.

"You won't need them," he told me.

I looked up the busy street. Cellie. *Call Cellie*. If I could get to a payphone, I could call collect.

I started my hobble. I knew that no one in the cars driving past had any idea what just happened. That my new husband had taken me on a kind of death drive through the city and then abandoned me on the street.

Cellie.

She had endured my rugged past alongside me, my tandem jumper on the leap. She had seen the multiple break-ups. Brian's wrath. Toward me, her, everything I deemed holy. Cellie knew the tears, the hours, the extrications, the returns.

She got it because we both had a bad ex-boyfriend. And though we had all the other things too: the same job and jokes, the same lust for fashion and theater, the same drama course and the same religion (Goddess worship and all that) we mostly aimed our spotlights on our terrible relationships.

Her ex was a one-time rocker, now fogey, 13 years her senior. I'd never met him, but I was acquainted with every fiery inch of their affair. And then the inexplicable bomb nine months in when he hurled himself into the arms of another woman for no apparent reason.

Cellie and I deconstructed our loves as if they were science or crucial, unburdening our hearts and trying to make sense of the nonsensical.

"Why," pleaded Cellie, "why would he write me a song with the lyric 'eternal love' in it, when clearly, our love is not eternal?"

Her eyes were as round as a Pierrot clown. Watery and desperate. I clutched her hand across the table. We usually performed our autopsies in dive bars or greasy spoons, over either cheap whiskey or cheap pie.

"Why?" she beseeched.

A terrible awe swept over me. As it does when truth crashes into light. This fact: men will say anything, anything at all. The force of women's hearts, their fact and ardor, are, irrelevant. Nothing. We are the contract, but are not a part of the contract. There are these types of men who will say anything and never mean it.

When I finally saw a picture of Cellie's ex, he was (of course) not at all like the rock star in our dreams. He was fat, unequivocally. Pasty. With a dyed black poodle perm. Stark bangs and long tresses. He was in his early thirties which was only notable because Cellie was just 19 when they met. I knew an actual adult had no business with someone so young. Why was Cellie wasting her time on this lothario?

It was perfectly clear to me that she was a modish angel. Cellie had long wavy hair that fell to her waist and the kind of pout people like to paint. She had an easy beauty, though that wasn't the best or the most of her. She was independent. She worked hard--at a few different waitress jobs. Had her own car and apartment. She had skedaddled from her oppressive Mennonite household the moment she turned 18, during her senior year in high school. And she hadn't needed any epiphanies about the family religion. There was no fall from grace because she had never bought tickets in the first place.

She used to wear a white lace baby doll gown from 1963, a super-mini, the kind of dress for a raucous bride. Her purse was another relic, made of stainless steel and shaped like a suitcase, Lilliputian and worn as a cross body. She put her hair up like Audrey Hepburn, lined her eyes in kohl and made me and the whole world laugh.

I saw that she was made of star flecks and bravery.

I was the only one who knew about the heartache. About the night she made off with her ex's garbage. Stole it from the curb and shuffled it up to the top of some parking tower. There she rummaged for clues about the new girlfriend. None were found: no used maxis or love notes. She told me how she had stuffed everything back into stretched plastic and tossed it off the fifth floor of the garage. Then she stared into the night, into a sorrow that would last decades, smoking her cigarette.

Meanwhile, I was in a cycle of leaving Brian and then returning. Which frustrated Cellie to pieces. She had always been my strongest advocate. She let me write her monologues that she performed with relish. She thought I was a fashion plate. She complimented my legs and nicknamed me "little butt," a contraindication to the fatness Brian diagnosed. You know how nervous I was to tell her I was going to marry him.

So I told her while she was frying up burgers. She worked at a brew pub and sometimes took a shift as line cook. My little fish in quicksand was wiggling. Squiggling. She gave me the same kind of look she must have given the dark sky on that garbage night. Then she went back to the fry station and flipped the burgers as if they were total jerks.

I ordered a beer and waited for her shift to end. Watching her slam the register, coins clanking. Acting like every customer was the profoundest nuisance on earth. Finally she was done and we walked together into the night. She bounded ahead of me, taking long strides down the middle of a street at midnight.

"Wait," I bellowed. "Aren't you even going to be happy for me?"

She turned with the kind of force I imagine attends witches in search of stolen cauldrons.

"Happy?" She screeched. "Happy?"

"I've been with you on this since the beginning. And I'll be with you until the end. When he crushes you, because he will. I will be there for you!"

Her eyes were wild with the helplessness of real love. "I will stand by you while you marry him."

Then she softened.

"But that man doesn't cherish you."

She said "cherish" like it was some kind of important word. She said it with music and urgency. Like it held the best and saddest keystrokes in every piano.

"He doesn't cherish you and he never will."

And then she walked over to me and took me by the arm.

"You don't have to," she whispered. But she knew that I would. I've always thought about that. Not about being cherished. I didn't understand that word at the time. Instead, I grabbed onto to the part about her standing by me. I was so relieved. Now I could go through with it. I wouldn't be alone. She would be there with me.

I didn't call her that night that Brian left me on the street. Two years later she would fly to my new city and extract me from Brian--for good this time. Paint the kitchen of the apartment I fled to. The worst apartment you ever saw.

"Aqua. Like you're in a swimming pool," smiled Cellie, up on the counter with a paint brush.

I had made it that one year without Brian in my life. That year of graduation and a new city, Cellie's city, and a job and graduate school.

Why did I call him again? What happened?

Cellie knew.

One night her roommate came over to my place. This guy. Our friend. All coked up. And he raped me. I fell backward into the sand. There was a tumult in our circle of friends. He had to move out of Cellie's. There wasn't any official reportage or anything like that. But I knew she wasn't surprised when I called Brian. She understood.

He uttered his proposal the first week we were back together.

I shivered inside the phone booth.

Cellie.

I knew how it would go. She would drop what she was doing. Drive over. Pick me up.

I would have to leave him. *But you're desperate to leave him.* That tickle. The fish of me flip-flopped. I shoved it under sand. I turned and limped the forty blocks home.

Brian was there lying on the living room floor. The huge t.v. set right next to him.

Soon after I would figure out that I was pregnant that night. Just a few weeks along. Too early to tell. In every possible way.

Brian and I would fight a lot over our baby's middle name. Our boy ended up with two. Because I wasn't giving in. One from Brian. One from me.

I chose Fisher. After my nudge, my fish. That light, that life inside me. Starting to break free.

THE FLIM-FLAM MAN

by Melissa Grossman

A high-falutin' flim-flam finagler, he was.
Flattery got him everywhere.
Sincere his words were,
but only in the moment.
Devilish, he was,
duplicitous in his diddling,
trifled with my affection, he did.
In vain I tried to tame him
gave him my heart, I did,
laid it on the table,
beside the mashed potatoes and gravy.
He took it all, 'cause he could.
Then moved on to my next-door neighbor.
Deceit only makes a man bolder, it does.

THE PROBLEM WITH GETTING FLOWERS

by Shay Cook

There are days when I arrive
home to roses, stems taller
than the love that wilts
within me. Glass blown
vases, banana leaf baskets,
and ornate bowls hold foliage
and buds that absorb life
and air from me.

And there are the handwritten
notes. Messages bleeding
from his ballpoint pen:
sorry, honey, sweetie, please,
hits me like the sharpness
of his fist against my jawbone,
like the thorn that pricks
my finger, extracting blood.

A LETTER TO HIS MISTRESS

by Jolene Hughes

Dear ____________,

I have mixed feelings about your affair with my husband.

On one hand, I feel a certain gratitude. He had been drunk daily for years and abusive to me daily for over a year before you two met. He'd keep me awake, yelling at me and breaking things and trying to kill himself and shaming me in drunken rages most nights until 1 or 2 in the morning. Treating me like I had cheated on him by having sex before we had met, although he had more previous partners than I. I got maybe 3 hours of sleep each night for a few years.

He kept a calendar to track the number of blowjobs he felt he was owed to compare it with the number he received. For years. I knew this behavior was rooted in pain and did my best to be empathetic and loving, but it was never enough. Eventually, I had to shut down emotionally in self-defense, and he decided to find someone else to fill his heart and bed. He recognized to a limited degree how awful he had been to me and the kids, and guilt overwhelmed him. He said he'd commit suicide if I didn't love him and forgive him for everything. So my feelings of gratitude are due to the fact that he didn't commit suicide because he had you in his bed and heart, thinking he walked on water and not immune to his considerable charm. My children still have a father because he found someone to love him when I couldn't.

On the other hand, instead of being a selfless true friend and making him fix the mess he made with his wife, you encouraged to direct his attention to you, to starting over emotionally in a new relationship with you. You are in love with my husband. I don't blame you; I was once, too. I'd like to be again. He refers to you as his surrogate for me, but considers you a better and more perfect lover. I dislike that term immensely. I would hope you do as well. He tells me you have been doing research into the custom, but there is no polyamory here: you are my husband's temporary, out-of-state mistress. His lover, not mine. No more, no less. I am not bisexual, but even if I were, a polyamorous three-person relationship with you would never happen. You interfered with my husband's attention on fixing the mess he made. You gave him hope that he could, but you have delayed and otherwise put challenges in the way of it actually happening.

You didn't cause trouble between us: he did. But your relationship is slowing down the rate of reconciliation between me and my husband. This, in turn, affects my children. I know, however, that nothing will change between you two as long as he is there with you. He's attached to you now and needs you too much for his happiness.

I know what it is like to make love with him. It is the delicious feeling of being worshipped, revered like Venus, and craved like a drug of which he can't get enough. I don't blame you for being addicted to that man. I have been addicted to him, too. You don't own him. I don't either. As the mother of his children and his wife, however, I outrank you in priority, if only legally, and knowing him for over 17 years (my entire adult life) affords me a deeper perspective on this man as opposed to your rather short relationship duration to date. Sometimes, to my great annoyance, I envy you as the recipient of his carefree love I should have had these past several months. I envy that you enjoy him at his best without being damaged by him.

I want him to continue to find his way home where he belongs, as should you, if you are his friend. I have suffered immense grief and heartbreak and abuse, yet am finding my way back to a place of love and forgiveness. I don't hold a grudge against you. Don't make it harder for him to fix the mess he's made than he and you and I already have. Don't make it harder for me to love and forgive him. Don't put demands on his time or attention beyond what he chooses to give you. I certainly understand how wonderful he can be. Even if you don't agree with that, surely you can understand how important it is that his young children have their two loving parents in a stable family unit.

Sincerely,

I was naive and wrong. None of this mess was her fault. She was a victim of his, too. A day came when I realized there could be no stable family unit as long as he was in it. He was no knight in shining armor who would come back and be gallant and save me. So I left him, and I saved myself and my children. And I apologized to her.

THE KILL

by Melissa Grossman

You were in control--overseeing everything, everyone.
You fed on fear; confidence threatened you.
One day you staged a brutal humiliation.
Piece by piece, you picked apart my artwork,
slyly smiling as you watched the shop light flicker out.
I stood there, incredulous. Gaping
at the shards of myself strewn around the room.
I could barely pull myself together.
But there you were,
strutting around the studio, euphoric -
blood on your hands.

MY SOUL

by Meaghan Andrews

My soul--breadcrumbs
--white once, now a fuzzy
blue,
black,
and grey.
Putrid lumps that lay on the ground, marking the trail
from where my journey started. Torn off
from where I had to sacrifice morsels of myself--
for a place to live,
for an education,
for the shackles of success--
I have become blackened. But there will be a day
when I leave you behind, and all the mold from my soul rots off.

BLUEBEARD, OR, THE IDEA OF EMILY

by Mo Daviau

Once upon a time, a man left a woman for me. I thought he was a prince, a prize. He swooped into my life and told me I was beautiful and special, and I believed him.

I did not ask him to leave his girlfriend for me. He told me he was polyamorous, and that meant that he could love both of us at the same time. I was going to meet her, and, with her blessing, he and I would wander off for intimate fun sexy times in a hotel room somewhere, then he'd go home to her.

When the opportunity to have him all to myself came along, I did not say no. I believed him when he said she was crazy, that he had had enough of her and the misery she brought him, that the very things that drew him to her in the first place now repelled him. She needed too much, and he couldn't, or wouldn't, provide. Soon after, girlfriend was gone, another on his list of exes, and I was swept up into the sea of his attention and adoration. It was intoxicating. At thirty-seven, I'd never felt anything as intensely romantic. I'd never in my life been made to feel so juicy, ecstatic, needed, or desired.

One day, a few months into our relationship, I went to his apartment. He had put a sexy painting of this ex that he had made while they were together on the wall of his living room. I said nothing about it. It was his apartment, after all, and he was an artist. A few weeks passed, and I finally said something about the fact that there was a sexy painting of her on the wall but not of me. "If it bothers you so much, I'll take it down," he yelled, not in embarrassment or misunderstanding, but in anger. This rattled me but I said nothing. He had made many sexy paintings of the woman before me but was holding out on doing a sexy one of me. I kept asking him when he would do a sexy painting of me, but he never answered the question. I felt ashamed for even asking. Then he told me he was going to do a sexy painting of another woman whose name kept coming up in conversation. I asked when he was going to do one of me. He looked at me and said nothing, and I knew I should be ashamed for asking.

Then, he left me for his next woman, but before he was done with me he told me he turned to her for comfort because I was depressed and I had asked him for help, and because of that, I was ruining his life. I don't know exactly what he said to this woman about me, but I imagine she was told that I was crazy, that I needed too much and he couldn't, or wouldn't, provide.

I left town. I lost my mind. For months, I had a panic attack every day. I blamed myself. I took meds. I went to therapy. The therapist told me I had done nothing wrong. I had been the victim of a man with Narcissistic Personality Disorder. A narcissist leaves a trail of women behind him, confused and blindsided, presenting with symptoms of PTSD. My therapist knew the name of the woman who came before me, since we talked about her all the time. Her name was Emily.

"He did the same thing to Emily," I would say to my therapist, but mostly to myself. I would cling to those words, to the idea of Emily, this woman who had suffered exactly as I was suffering. That there were other women out in the world that he had charmed and harmed was proof that I wasn't crazy or insecure or the horrible girlfriend he told me I was. And I had proof that he had done the same to her.

Emily had written about his discarding of her. I stalked her social media one night on the couch while one of my friends kept an eye on me to take sure I didn't hurt myself. I was looking for answers, a sign that maybe if she was okay, then I could be, too. Instead, I found an essay she had written about his abandoning her and going to me. About how he refused to help her when she told him she was suicidal and needed his help. About how he left her crying on the floor of the apartment they shared, begging him to help her. About how cold he was when he refused, turned his back on her, and left. About how he left her crying and scared in order to walk down to the park to call me, unaffected by her pain, fully present for another sexy, flirty phone call.

I showed her essay to my therapist. "See!" It was the canonical text that made me stop blaming myself for what had happened, that clicked my brain over to accepting that he had abused me, because he had abused her.

I wanted to write to Emily to thank her for putting that essay online. I'd read it a hundred times or more, over and over, like scripture, as I struggled to accept that I had been abused, he was abusive, he had abused other women before me. My therapist didn't think it was a good idea. I might be bothering her. She might be in a good place now and not want to rehash all the abuse and torment. Or, from what I had been told about her by our mutual ex, she wasn't a very nice or warm person. She probably wouldn't want to help me. I was the other woman, and she didn't owe me shit.

I wrote her a note and sent it, not expecting her to respond. But she did.

I was on a shift at the bookstore where I worked when her email landed in my inbox. I ran to the restroom to read it. She didn't sound horrible and crazy at all. She said she was sorry that he had hurt me as he had hurt her, and wished there was a way to stop him from hurting others.

I didn't write back to thank her for that e-mail, the e-mail that changed the game of my recovery because I didn't want to bother or upset her. She wasn't my friend, after all, and I had no business trying to make her my friend. Who becomes friends with the woman their ex left them for? Nobody.

Seven months after this, when I moved back to Portland, I ran into Emily at a reading in a bar. I had been hoping to run into her. I was the woman our mutual abuser had used to make her feel bad about herself. I couldn't just call her and say "hey, I'm back in town, thank you for that e- mail seven months ago, you prevented me from jumping in front of a truck, let's hang out sometime." I didn't think I could ask this woman for friendship. She could be a compassionate human being by telling me that, yes, it happened to her, too, sorry, I wish you well, or she could have ignored me or told me to fuck off. Any of those would have been acceptable responses.

If I had any doubt left over what had happened to us, about naming what he did to us abuse, they evaporated when I finally did run into her. The unspoken knowledge of a shared sisterhood wrapped around us like vines. She didn't need to say a word as we looked into each other's eyes, and neither did I. Her energy screamed, yes! me too.

"Do we need to go have a drink?" I nodded. We had a drink.

In the European folk tale Bluebeard, a young woman and her two older sisters are courted by a wealthy, grandiose man whose beard is the strange color of indigo. This man is charming and bestows upon the sisters many gifts. Bluebeard creeps out the two older sisters; it's the youngest one who accepts his offer of marriage. She feels sorry for him--his beard is blue, after all, and he seems a little sad about it. He's an older man, and has been married several times before, but no one seems to question why his wives keep disappearing. He is given the benefit of the doubt at all times, and even seems a little pathetic, what with that bizarre blue beard.

He moves her into his castle, and one night, after they are married, he is called away on business. He gives her the keys to every room in the castle. One key, the tiniest one, opens a room that Bluebeard forbids his wife from entering. After he's gone, the girl and her sisters look inside every room in the house, including the one she was told not to enter. The three sisters don't even think that there might be evil ahead for them. They fling open the forbidden door without a thought to Bluebeard. There, she sees that this room is where her husband keeps the corpses of his former wives, rotting and decapitated, their blood pooled on the floor.

That the tiny key in the palm of her hand was covered in blood, proves that she has crossed Bluebeard. That she knows his darkest secret. Bluebeard returns home early and sees his guilty bride with the bloody key in the palm of her hand. As he prepares to add her to his collection of dead wives, the young woman's two brothers appear out of nowhere and cut off Bluebeard's head with their swords.

The tale of Bluebeard is the first archetypical story that Clarissa Pinkola Estes, in her classic book *The Women Who Run With the Wolves*, dissects. Her analysis of the archetypes in this story are not wrong: that women are taught to override their intuition from a very young age in order to be kind and accommodating, and that their hunger and curiosity for the truth will get them into dangerous situations at least a few times in their lives. That there are men out there who embody the Bluebeard archetype, each of them promising the sweetness of romance to women but ending with the woman without her head in some way, locked in the bloody chamber, while another woman holds in the key.

Nowhere in this book does Clarissa Pinkola Estes chastise the older sisters for not pulling the youngest one aside and saying, "Holy shit, this Bluebeard guy is bad news. He's a creeper! Don't marry him!" The girl who falls into his trap has to learn for herself, by which I mean be rescued by men. No one seems to think it's wrong or strange that the older sisters' gut reaction to Bluebeard was right but overlooked, or that the older sisters said nothing. Because, really: would the youngest sister, so charmed by this big, odd-looking man, thinking he could love her as she could love him, have believed them?

In another version of the story, Emily would have found me on Facebook and written me a note and told me that she'd been emotionally flayed by this man she loved. That's he'd killed her soul and strung her up in his bloody chamber.

In another version of the story, Emily would have found me on Facebook and told me that she had seen his cruelty firsthand, and to run like hell. And I would have thanked her and run and saved myself from him.

In another version of the story, she would have warned me.

"But would you have believed me?" she asked. A reasonable question.

There's a reason that not even a feminist writer like Clarissa

Pinkola Estes doesn't find the fault in the Bluebeard story to be in the failure of the older sisters to tell the younger one not to marry that strange man with the blue beard.

When I tell you that I'm okay, that I'm mostly healed from what our abuser, who I truly was in love with, did to me, you have to realize there's still a part of me that's hanging dead in his bloody chamber. And that there's another woman out there with him now, so charmed, who will soon enough find a bloody key in her hand.

And there's the matter of my half-assed attempt at warning her. A post on my blog, which I knew she was reading. I wrote that I wanted to help her see that a man whose last three girlfriends were left suicidal and traumatized needed to consider that he was the common denominator. I told her I wished the best for her. I told her I hoped that she truly was the different, special one.

Would I have believed anyone at that time, my head so full of stars and lies and promises of great love and connection?

I've spent a lot of time thinking about this one. Even after everything I've been through, worked on, thought about, written about, ran past my therapist, the honest answer is, probably not.

European folk tales are malleable, rewritable, and way, way out of copyright. So here, I present a new variation: With Bluebeard dead and his widow spared, she and her older sisters, the ones who thought he was bad news and didn't want to marry him, go to a bar and celebrate their survival with whiskey. The sisters are anxious to hear what had happened to their younger sister. Into the bar walks another woman. Another woman who got away and didn't end up in the bloody chamber. She and the widow lock eyes. They don't need to use words. The energy that emanates from their bodies, the compassion and wisdom in each of their eyes shows the other yes, her too. The girl walks away from her sisters and embraces the other woman, her survivor-sister. For theirs is a connection that is so strong and so strange that other people warn her not to trust it. For a woman alone pointing to a man and crying "abuse" knows she will be called crazy, or that she cannot be trusted to tell her own story. Two women pointing to the same man crying abuse? Well, that's a little dangerous. Three women? Four?

The women who hang as corpses in his bloody chamber lift their eyes, reborn. They are butterflies, phoenixes, ghosts. They are equal parts frightening and beautiful. They don't seek revenge. They don't need it. They have each other.

As Emily and I drank and drew the lines between our experiences and unwound the lies we had been told, I worried that I was using her, or running the risk of retraumatizing her. I told her to tell me if she didn't want to talk about him or the abuse he dealt us. She promised she would but never did.

I told her I would have understood if she hadn't wanted to talk to me at all. I was, after all, the bright and shiny new thing that a man she loved used as a pawn to make her feel shitty about herself. But in getting to know her, I see how horrible it is when women continue to let men control the conversation and their own versions of reality. Emily is in no way the sullen, angry harpy he insisted she was. His recasting her as a lousy girlfriend whose depression was making his life miserable was merely his gambit to get me interested, to justify his dumping her and swiftly taking up with me. The sad story of his life as an outsider weirdo was meant to align with my own. Love-bombing. Mirroring. And then it quickly slipped away, and he gutted me, and only later, when I was damn near dead, did I see that there was a bloody key in my hand all along. And that I hadn't been saved by my metaphorical brothers, but by Emily.

"He really is Bluebeard," Emily said once, and I said yes.

Women who have survived abusive men know that a lot of people won't believe them. That others will shame their mouths closed and tell them that they run the risk of being seen as a "crazy ex." We tell women that they will never be seen as reliable witnesses to their own lives. We silence them with accusations of bitterness and jealousy. We remind them that there was something unattractive about them that must have made him leave.

In all of this, women forget that other women can be our helpers, our saviors, and our friends. To refuse to listen to a woman when she warns you her ex is an asshole or an abuser or anything between is to say that men are always right and women are always suspect.

Or, as Rebecca Solnit, who's far wiser than me, once wrote:

> "Not uncommonly, when a woman says something that impugns a man, particularly a powerful one (not a black one unless he's just been nominated for the Supreme Court by a Republican president), or an institution, especially if it has to do with sex, the response will question not just the facts of her assertion but her capacity to speak and her right to do so. Generations of women have been told they are delusional, confused, manipulative, malicious, conspiratorial, congenitally dishonest, often all at once."
>
> --Rebecca Solnit, "Cassandra Among the Creeps"

People have let us know that they think it's weird that we're friends. We note all the time, the guy who abused us has great taste in women. Emily and I have a lot in common. We'd be friends even if we'd met in a less dramatic way.

In another version of the story, I killed myself and Emily heard about it through the grapevine, and she sunk to the floor of her bedroom one night and cried because she felt that her story could have saved me.

In a version of the story I hope I never hear, his current victim kills herself and Emily and I hear about it through the grapevine, and we cry because our story couldn't save her.

There is no version of the story where Emily told me to fuck off, where we never met and became the friend we needed to prove that the other one wasn't crazy, where she or I went off the deep end, such that we are not here to tell our story.

In the version of the story that is true, I lose part of my soul and my brain takes a beating, but I also make a new friend, one who reminds me that other women are our friends and saviors, never the competition that men want us to believe they are.

THE EYES OF SOUL

by Ayesha Fayyaz

I fear people with insight of depth, trauma, and divinity. The kind of people who can look into your eyes and jump into your soul. I fear because I know how much of a terrible being I am. The crushed, foul-smelling, stabbed, bleeding soul. The scars. The smoke and ashes in place of heart, I mean the suffocation; the breathlessness. The exhaustion. The constant war of empathy and apathy. The isolation and worthlessness. The high-pitched devious screams. The toxicity of narcissists. The prolonged coma. The terribleness. I fear because such people take my breath away. They get to know all-of-me and still be calm on surface. The lava rises but keeps eyes hypnotized. The power and the powerlessness. Then I realized its power as I can see through them too. It's war of energies then. It's I- know-you type of energy and it's okay to exist. It's okay to be uncomfortable among my type of people, the comforting type. Because everyone is highly comfortable within his/herself. It's okay to have an intimate connection without even wanting it. It's universal, it's natural. Like some writers connect with the readers in the very first line, some people connect with us in the very first sight. We have no inhibition to this.

HOMEWARD BOUND

by Rehana Campbell

I feel uprooted,
Although it isn’t a foreign feeling.
I’ve tasted the unknown plenty,
And ever so gently absorbed its meaning.
The seemingly single source of solitude stiffens your jaw,
But I must tell you to unthaw,
Spread roots to inner most thoughts.
They’ll dance over you like a trickling stream,
They’ll cling to you like sticky whipped cream,
They’ll mingle with you, soft yet supreme.
When the mind lets go of worries untold,
Of juries in control,
Of furies blizzard cold,
Peace sets in.
The expanding orange mist glides over the pink dusk,
Sparkling with each brushstroke of lust.
Sensations of all kinds enter my realm,
And let them in I must.
This was always my home,
But now I am aware of it.
This was always my home,
But now I am conscious of it.

BRUSH FIRES AND BAD THERAPY

by Julie Butler

She sat across from me in an overstuffed easy chair, with one foot tucked under her bottom and the other slippered foot dusting the floor. She creased her brow and nodded compassionate *m-hmm*'s while I spoke.

When my story concluded, she blinked slowly and deliberately. Her hands met in prayer position and she inhaled deeply. "The midlife years are really all about growth," she nodded. "This is a wonderful opportunity to weed your garden."

My heart sunk at the horticultural metaphor. She was the fifth counsellor I had seen. I had pinned my hope to her ability to understand what I said and perhaps intuit all that I could not articulate. Her response seemed like such an obvious, cheap and easy platitude. Yes, life is about growth, yet there was nothing in my recent history that I could relate to the pastoral scene she painted. I was not a woman in a wide-brimmed hat with a trug slouching at her elbow, casually pulling dandelions amid the roses in a pastel, English garden.

No, I was in a brush fire.

My dad was a gardener... rather, a pretend-farmer. A displaced prairie boy. He did his best to flavour my suburban upbringing with his own childhood experiences. My older brother and I sat between garden rows on overturned buckets with our backs bent low against the merciless summer sun, and a carpet of creeping weeds before us. He told us about the summer wildfires that did his weeding for him.

His early years in Saskatchewan were marked by Depression era drought; the wheat fields were a dustbowl. Hot July winds rolled across the Badlands over the parched land gathering the ghosts of once fertile earth into dark, gritty clouds. Heat lightening or a careless, errant spark would occasionally ignite the fields of golden stubble and the winds would fan the first cinders into orange tongues. The fiery front could consume an arid meadow in minutes, smoke and flames leapfrogging each other with each lick of the breeze.

One such fire raced towards the small cabin my father called home. His parents were away and the sentinel of airborne ash only gave enough warning to collect his two brothers, their dog and a few household items. They pitched their belongings hurriedly into the slew and tumbled in after them.

In those dry days, the slew, an irrigation pond beyond the shed was reduced to a muddy ditch rank with decomposing vegetation. The dog had to be persuaded to lower its body into the putrid shallows. They sank low into the murk as the crackle of fire approached, hearing the pop and whine of flames overtaking the cabin timbers. They pressed themselves lower still, as flashes of orange reached out over their heads toward the far bank and grey smoke filled the hollow of the slew.

The boys huddled close until the intensity of the heat receded and the air cleared. The grassy parapet was a ragged ridge of charred turf and smoldering ground. They climbed the steep slope up and stood side-by- side to survey what remained. The cabin was a blackened mound of charcoal; even the fieldstone chimney had toppled. The shed was little more than a smear punctuated by jagged iron remnants of tools. Where the vegetable garden had once been, their tin bucket was still there, upside-down and blackened. The plants, the grove of trees and all acreage in sight were dead.

This perspective was relatable. Pulling myself from the toxic relationship was like leaving the slew, something familiar though nauseating, and stepping up into a barren, new world. Everything I knew had been consumed in my ex's destructive path. The things that weren't burnt entirely to the ground, wiped clear out of existence but for a dirty smudge on my memory, were so saturated by the experience, they were rendered worthless. The pain in emerging was all-sensory; there was not a smell nor sound that did not trigger recollection of some moment of confusion or exploitation. His ash had fallen absolutely everywhere and his manipulations were like fumes in my lungs that could not be exhaled.

I studied her face, kind yet so dispassionate. I could guess what was coming. The irony was, the sage advice that would probably follow, would be words my pathological partner had said with feigned empathy and a paper-thin remorse for having hurt me in our breakup. He also condescendingly described it as an opportunity. I could focus on myself; I had been entirely too invested in his life and had abandoned my own. These wise words were hard to hear as he left out the parts about the subtlety of his psychological games and how they had slowly teased my intuition, judgment and self-respect away from me. He had been perpetually burdened by crises and injustices, the victim of an embittered, unstable ex from whom he needed protection. The ruse was an excellent way to detour and derail my energies and attention.

He did not administer a sharp discard, but instead slyly introduced me to triangulation. I was supposed to love him enough to accept his soulful explorations with the petite blonde, coupled with declarations that I was truly the One. He toyed with my competitive nature and hunger to believe his regretful tears. He stoked his own brush fire in my heart and mind, for the pleasure and power in it. He then dropped a lit match into the environment he prepared so perfectly, and watched the combustion. There was chiding, blaming, and denying any accountability, while privately, the breadth of his destructive impact was his rapture.

I wondered often if it was by design and strategy or by innate genius, that he managed such a comprehensive and personalized undermining of my self-worth and ability to heal. When I tried to exercise, did he know how I replayed his belittling words about my excess weight or my excess vanity in wanting to shed it? Did he know that I could not paint a stroke in the studio, while I ruminated on his confusing accusations that I had only started painting to antagonize his ex? When I sought solace in meditation or spiritual reading, did he imagine how his whispered personal dogma, borrowed from Buddhism, psychology and modern philosophy and twisted to his liking, tampered with my best efforts?

Of course, his sabotage was overt as well. He had taken pains to spread out tendrils and choke out the support of my closest relationships, smearing, lying, massaging their weaknesses to his advantage, and creating alienation and a suffocating isolation. My reputation, public standing and career were all handy kindling for his deviant appetite for domination. When humiliating me, he spared no ground.

I squinted back at the therapist. Was she even looking at me? I felt as though I had been moving through the world for months beneath a cascade of physical symptoms of trauma. They were so incapacitating and overwhelming to me, I assumed they were as obvious to observers. My hair had fallen out in handfuls, insomnia marked dark circles under my eyes, psychosomatic neuropathy weighed down my right foot so I limped into her office. I was pale, twitching with anxiety, and my eyes were dull and distracted. Under my blouse, my heart beat out random arrhythmias and I was recovering from shingles; only the most recent in a series of autoimmune ailments. I felt the stress ring my neck muscles, and I suddenly was repulsed by the slant of her eyebrows, her upholstery, and the framed poster on her wall.

The old, unsinged me would have stayed for the balance of the hour, grudgingly written her a cheque, and suppressed the inclination to decline booking another session. I would have returned the following week and attempted to explain myself better so that she could maybe understand and not chase my descriptions of trauma with invalidating *m-hmm*'s.

"You don't get it," I said, and left her cozy office, without any further explanation or justification. How could she? We are not conditioned to see pathology. We cannot live with the thought that our very souls are flammable and loving the disordered can deliver devastation on par with natural disaster. I could not spend another minute in futility, attempting to make the inconceivable known.

That was growth. That was one weed plucked.

CHILD, LIKE ME

by Rehana Campbell

The struggle wraps around my throat like ropes, twisting and choking.
Dark light enters my eyes and my own lightness dims,
Where have I gone?

Back to my dark universe,
The one I set up so well.
Walls painted with fantasies, desires and hopes,
Carpeted floors cushioning egos, but I remember all of their footprints.
I'll always remember.
Happiness must always come at a price.
Because I had my dark universe and it was mine, they wanted to consume it.
It wasn't enough for them that I only existed in codes and equations, They needed to consume it.
Cannibalistic manipulations draining me of my blood...
Might I be tastier?

LUCID DREAM

by Meaghan Andrews

I had a dream that
I killed myself--
Unyielding metal
to penetrate my skull,
a permanent silence to
What's wrong?
that *Nothing*
could no longer fill.
Running for miles
on cold asphalt,
unnoticed.
Until suddenly--
bodies everywhere, crowding
in a sea of flesh and bone
and eyes. They screamed
Do it! and as the shot
sounded they laughed.

GUILTY

by Kristen Polito

Feeling guilty has been a predominant theme in my life. As a child, I learned to feel guilty about eating, ashamed about my body and, for some reason, responsible for my family's collective happiness.

I often felt at fault; just in the wrong somehow. This could be attributed to the prevailing anxiety disorder which made its presence known around the age of five. It could also have something to do with the way my mother operated. She rarely doled out praise and, when she did, it was underscored with some sort of veiled reprimand. In her book, there was always room for improvement.

When I came in first runner-up at the Little Miss Flagler County pageant at the age of seven she rationalized the reason for my "loss" as my being considerably larger than the winner: a tiny and adorable girl named Maven.

To be clear, she did not say outright that I was large, but that the other girl was very small, and that was why she won. I thus inferred my relative size to be the problem. Additionally, she made some grumbling remarks about small-town nepotism on the judging panel that I didn't quite understand at the time.

As I got older, there were additional instances where my size proved to be my downfall and hindered me from progressing in activities which my mom had championed. I felt guilty for growing too tall for gymnastics, and I was just too awkward to be light on my feet in tap and ballet.

I wanted to be small like my friends; tiny. I equated smallness with thinness and thinness with value. I greatly disliked being the large, beastly giant amongst my pixie-sized girlfriends. I towered. I felt like Lurch from The Addams Family most of the time. I wanted to shrink into myself. I wanted to fit into my friends' clothes so we could share. I wanted to fit in.

When I was in middle school, I befriended a very beautiful girl named Stacy. Stacy had blonde hair, blue eyes and could give Heather Graham a run for her money. Upon meeting her, my mom was immediately enamored of her. While Stacy and I were growing up and becoming interested in boys, my mother always expressed disdain for the dating choices Stacy made. *Stacy should be a model. Stacy shouldn't settle for this person or that person. Stacy looked just like Heather Graham!* She was like a broken record. Yes, my friend was (and is) very beautiful.

I agreed with everything she said about my friend, but this friendship dynamic triggered the same feelings of inadequacy by comparison. It's wearying to the soul after a while.

Stacy and I had a falling out in high school, but then became roommates later in college. However, by this time, I was very ill with my first major bout of anorexia and I was unable to foster any sort of human connection, even with my former best friend.

Years later, Stacy and I were still in touch, just not as close as we once were. Stacy, normal and well-adjusted, had married and had children: two beautiful girls and a boy. My mom's laser focus praise for Stacy suddenly turned to Stacy's children who "absolutely had to get into modeling and acting." Soon she was emailing Stacy with all sorts of unsolicited information on exactly what she should do with her beautiful babies: links and contact names for people in the biz.

Stacy is pretty level-headed when it comes to her kids. She's got them enrolled in plenty of activities, but they are character-building, and none of them have anything to do with appearance. The girls are in soccer and take piano lessons. One of the older girls' skateboard. The boy, who's the youngest, is super-smart and already spelling independently on his iPad. I had begun to feel guilty, worrying that maybe the "helpful suggestions" might seem appealing and wind up damaging the kids in the long run.

However, I quickly realized that worry was unfounded. Stacy is not my mother, and seeing how easily she ignored her suggestion was kind of empowering to me in a way. How did she do that? I've always felt trapped, as though I've had no say. Either go with the "suggestion" or wrestle with that sick feeling of guilt in the pit of my stomach.
Is it possible for me to let go of guilt and still act autonomously?

I can pay attention to my own wish to get rid of guilty feelings. I can keep my own needs and the needs of the other people in my life in my mind. I can forgive myself for wanting happiness.

Happiness.

That's one thing I don't have to feel guilty about.

NEVER YOU

by Mandy Waysman

I never want to be you
I never want to set eyes on the sickening view
I never want to smell your stench of agony
Or see the signs you peg on those like me

I never want to learn how to manipulate
How's this for something to contemplate
Though I have been close to ending it all
I did not give you a front seat to my fall

I do not have pride in much
But this does me good in a crunch
I have seen you lose it more than once
Have watched as you yell madly, you dunce

Angry words and hateful names
Spoken to the ones from whence you came
Though I wish I had the power to hate you
I ask god to make the pains of your fate few

I can't spit the venom of the crude
For that would make me just like you
Because of you I strived to be perfect
This legacy leads me to never fit

Do you know I will always be your biggest fan
Even though I don't know who I am
I pray you never see the pain you caused
I will never admit the hope has been lost

I used to look up to you and saw you as worthier
But you continued to slip away further
I wonder If you will see your flaws
I will spell out without much pause

As children, you were bright and funny
Never afraid to play the dummy
Years passed and you became fake
Never wanting to show you cared or claimed a stake

You began to be ever more involved with yourself
Letting those you loved clutter the shelf
When you needed money, food, or home
Or just to feel not so alone

We were there to pick you back up
Tears of thankfulness, not one drop
Never good enough were we
Or maybe it was just me

Do tell what magic can be performed
To bring back the one who was so charmed
I could never be like you
could never be heartless enough to take your cue

Do I wait for you around the bend
or just say so long to one who was like kin
Will this writing hit the mark
or will it haunt others, pushing them further into the dark

ILLUSIONS

by Rehana Campbell

Satin ribbons caress my hips,
Lacing my thighs,
Wrapping around my calves and spiraling into existence.
A pulsating velvet glow expands throughout my chest,
Is it best to unstitch and show you the source?
Perhaps not.
Perhaps I shall walk into the horizon and blend into a thousand rays of sunlight.
I want to spread my wings and glide with the world winds,
They whirlwind through a fabric of solar systems,
Shimmering layers of wisdom onto the Earth,
Awakening eyes to the mirror in the sky.

I will dip my toes into the pond of perishment,
Until I am no more and no more is all there is to be.
Sandpaper lips take flight and crack into a smile.
Being will cradle me back into existence,
Where I'll always be.
The loving unity of my infinity,
Strongly whispers what I already knew lifetimes ago.

I WISH PEOPLE CAME WITH SUBTITLES

by Kristen Polito

I hardly ever get the opportunity to see all of my brothers at once, so when two of the oft-absent siblings were recently in town, I made the extra effort to go see them at my dad's house where they'd be crashing for the weekend.

When I first arrived, I noticed a movie playing in the family room with the closed caption feature enabled. Naturally, this version displays subtitles at the bottom of the screen, providing viewers the words to the entire episode. I could see and hear it from the foyer: a popular actress was lighting up the screen and deftly stealing the heart of her co-star while every last word was accounted for.

I remarked to no one in particular that I have a habit of utilizing the subtitle feature on absolutely everything I watch, without exception. Literally, it is unreservedly compulsive. I detest watching movies or television without this feature and, if said option is not available, its absence becomes so distracting that I will often cease watching altogether. I'm so used to doing it, that, when I don't, I feel as though I'm missing one of my senses-like the sound is turned all the way down on the program, even though I know, of course, that it's not.

I'm not sure when the obsessive subtitles dependency began, but I can definitively say that I have been doing it for the last 5 years minimum. The inclination toward doing this probably originated simultaneously with my Netflix binge-watching habit.

In response to my comment, my brother agreed that he's likewise fond, verging-on-obsessed with subtitles. I know my mom uses subtitles at her house, too. She's big on foreign cinema. Also, she utilizes the feature while running on her treadmill because that can get noisy.

It could be that my family members and I are genetically predisposed towards auditory issues, but that explanation seems unlikely. Rather, I believe that our collective devotion to reading, both for pleasure and education, is so strong that we simply prefer to "read" what we watch. As a child, I had a strong and enduring passion for reading. I sought it out as an "escape" and a comfort. As an adult, I still seek relief in its familiarity.

I wish I could apply the comfort and familiarity of the "Subtitle Feature" to my life; especially when interacting with people in real life.

And dogs, too, that would be neat. So entertaining.

But as far as human interactions are concerned, subtitles would be incredibly useful, because, let me tell you, I really suck at reading a room. By using subtitles, I'd be able to tell when my oldest brothers are teasing me or being just plain mean. With subtitles, the inscrutable thoughts and feelings of my youngest autistic brothers would be made plain. Their speech apraxia would no longer be a communication deterrent.

Moreover, talking to my parents would be simplified. I'd assuredly know if, during a conversation, my stoic mother was expository or encouraging in that particular moment. Theoretically, reading her emotions would provide guidance on how to navigate each and every interaction.

Likewise, subtitles would provide a better interpretation of my father's reactions to information and events. I'd gain entree into what lies past his unreadable expressions, which are reserved for the difficult conversations, and thus be advised when to share freely versus when to filter.

It would really clarify things.

But without having those subtitles to fall back on, I find that when it comes to my parents' feedback specifically, it's best for them to be vague. I can't help but bear the impact of their opinion, so, if things are to remain copacetic, it needs to be a fairly ambiguous one.

Perhaps most adult children experience this, or a similar dynamic with one or both of their parents. It's difficult making that transition from child to adult; especially when that child is complicated and floundering. My public writing is often intense and occasionally results in controversial feedback. In providing "subtitles" for my message here, allow me to say that I am truly grateful to have an outlet to freely express myself and my feelings.

If subtitles were optional on human interactions, would you use them or just "wing it"?

BREAKING UP, 1957

by Jeanie Greensfelder

She stood in the wood and glass phone booth,
dialed the operator, deposited coins, and watched
classmates cross campus for breakfast.

He answered, and she said,
I called to say goodbye.
We need to break up.

He would not listen: she had turned eighteen,
he had gotten his divorce, he was driving up,
they'd elope today, she'd be his wife.

She hung up, slumped down
and sat on her heels in the booth.
Having failed to say goodbye,

she became a star in a drama,
one where he wrote the script
and directed her performance.

Wanting her family to suffer,
she used to imagine her funeral.
Now she'd get to watch.

A version of this poem was published in *Biting the Apple*, Pencilled In, 2012

GIVE AND TAKE

by Catherine Wald

She
gave me everything
        but took away
                more

fed me on poisoned
        apples after pricking
                me with spindles

compressed my diaphragm
        shackled my tongue
                tainted my breath

put serpents in my ears
        fed my heart to frogs
                duct-taped every opening

acted as if she had a right

THE FULL MOON IN AN EMPATH

by Ayesha Fayyaz

And here I was
Waiting to watch
The rising
the grand rising
Of full moon in me
Though deleterious
But I had no inhibition
To cosmic beauty of its charm
Its storm
its celestial perfection
Of imperfection
Though erode my scars
But I fall every time, break my colours
For this magnetic narcissist
As a product
misery melts from the roots of my hair
Lingers on tips
Lingers like a monster's presence
Pulling my hair
My skin bleeding and shedding terribly
Revealing stab wounds of my soul
At this destruction I can't handle myself
I am vulnerable yet disastrous
I am intense
I crave more misery
I am not satisfied with enough
Like a roaring ocean ______
Craving to touch moon.

MY SLEEPING GIANT

by Rehana Campbell

The body is a field of sensation,
With prickles and tingles,
Those overlapping waves of guilt, anxiety and shame.
It is not a hostile place, although it may seem,
It is my home filled with memories, both seen and unseen.
Like patchwork, disorganized patterns were stitched carelessly,
From a past where careless me would sit lazily.
"You are unworthy and useless,"
Her words filled my capillaries, pumping doubt and insecurity,
Clouded moments evolving a foggy identity.
One morning I created space,
Placing a finger to my third eye, the forgotten came to light,
Bringing with it a warm viscosit glow,
Soothing the grooves and canals of my weathered soul.
Now a pink illuminating river flows within,
Carrying thoughts that reawaken.
My sleeping giant: so bold and so vascular,
Just waiting for me to rescue her.

GYPSY'S

by Julie Guirgis

I saw his car pull up, but he hadn't noticed me. I knocked on the wood paneled doors of his home, detected his silhouette through the closed blinds, and the shadow of his hair behind the door frame. Shouting like a madwoman I cried out, "I'm not going anywhere until you answer the door you scumbag!" He made no effort to come to the door; he merely continued to hide like the coward he was. I ripped the metal screen in a frenzied rage and kept banging until my knuckles were red and sore. Then I started kicking the door screaming "I hate you, you fucker, you're nothing but a piece of shit. You haven't seen the last of me." He hid...I left drained and exhausted.

I first met him at Gypsy's cafe; a haven for artists of all kinds: musicians, artists, writers and poets. As I sat down in a quiet corner to sketch designs I noticed someone staring at me from the corner of my eye. Curious, I looked around, trying not to appear too obvious. I saw a man in his forties wearing a studded leather jacket, stonewash jeans, and a Guns n' Roses t-shirt. His hooded gray blue eyes mixed with blue eyeliner made him look almost pretty.

"I like your shirt," I blurted. I hadn't dated for a while and was a little rusty when it came to approaching men.

"Yeah, they're pretty cool," he replied casually. He had a voice that I couldn't imagine raised. I got so turned on when he tousled his long bleached blond hair and pursed his lips like he was Brett Michaels, the lead singer from Poison. Sexy bad-boy types always got my attention.

He sat down near me, and carefully removed his electric guitar from its case, cradling it like a baby.

"What's your favorite Gunners song?, " he asked.

"Estranged."

"Good pick."

When he started to play the room became still. The haunting sound delicately penetrated some long-forgotten place within me. I stood with eyes closed savoring the magnificence of the moment. When I opened my eyes I discovered that I wasn't his only fan. Female admirers buzzed around him wide-eyed and animated.

"You're a great musician, thanks for playing that for me."

"I'm Julie by the way."

"My name's Harley."

"Do you have a Harley, Harley?" I joked.

"Actually I do. Maybe I'll take you for a spin sometime," he said with a grin. I felt like he had already taken me for a spin...being around him made me feel light-headed. I liked the way he spoke with an air of mystery. His cool persona attracted me. He was a puzzle I yearned to solve.

"I'll take you up on that, see you round," I said, then left. Unlike the other women, I wanted to play hard to get.

A couple of weeks later I went to Gypsy's to see if Harley was there. On arrival I noticed a Harley Davidson parked outside, and hurried in. I spotted him with a new batch of groupies; with mascara coated on as thick as a caterpillar, and enough hairspray on their heads to protect them from Russian bombs. I walked past him towards the counter and ordered a coffee hoping he would see me.

"Hey Julie I owe you a ride," Harley called out.

"Oh yeah, I forgot about that," I lied, trying to act nonchalant. "I'll just have my coffee and meet you outside." The women glared at me, exposing their jealousy. Unfazed by it, I ignored them.

I swung one leg over the smooth leather seat, resting my foot on the side pedal. My small frame shadowed his muscular physique, my arms wrapped around his lean waist, and my hands locked across his strong stomach. I closed my eyes and leaned into him, resting my face on his back, inhaling the musk of his body - a mixture of sweat, cologne, and tobacco.

When I was young I liked to party. My motto was I'll try anything once, twice if I like it. From the age of fourteen, smoking pot after school became part of my staple diet, followed by popping pills. I dated a guy who stole and forged scrips for a living. His door was always open until the early hours of the morning and closed shut the day he got nabbed for forgery. By the age of nineteen I graduated to heroin, the perfect high.

My boyfriend placed the drug paraphernalia on the dirty brown carpet adorned with cigarette burns. He grabbed the spoon, and tipped some smack in it. The white powder shone like tiny crystals. Adding a few drops of water to mix he sucked up the potion with the needle, as I strapped on a tourniquet in search of a vein.

"Just a little pinprick honey," he said with a devilish grin.

I immediately laid back as the warm sensation surged through me. I felt like I was wrapped in a soft blanket, lulled in my mother's arms, floating in the ether.

"Man, this shit is good!" For a couple of years heroin encased me in a little cotton wool house where nothing hurt anymore. I was blissfully numb.

Coming home late into the night or disappearing for days were not uncommon for me. Already slender, I looked gaunt and showed signs of addiction. I wore sweaters even on hot days to hide my pin cushioned arms.

Sometimes while strung out in a hazy blur I would see my mother kneeling and quietly sobbing, praying to God to save her lost little girl.

"Promise me you will get help," my mom pleaded. I blinked back tears when I saw mom in pain. But if I was honest I was torn between the love I had for my mom and my opiate romance. One day I returned home after a two day binge still strung out, with disheveled clothing and hair resembling a bird's nest. My mother was crying in the driveway while men carried my dad onto a stretcher, wheeling him into the ambulance.

Dad had suffered a heart attack. "Taking medication and regular visits to the cardiologist are important but so is avoiding stress," the doctor ordered. I knew my reckless lifestyle was a contributing cause to my father's decline. Not only did I feel compelled to make peace with my father on earth but with my father in heaven. I knew I had been given a second chance, and if I didn't quit now I never would. Wrestling with a tough decision, I left my boyfriend and checked into a rehab with a twelve step program.

Although when I met Harley I was a Christian and twelve years drug- free, I still had a weakness for the tough boys. "I guess old habits die hard," I shrugged.

Harley was the eldest of three brothers and his mother's golden boy. He attended a music conservatory as a child learning to play the piano, violin, and guitar. Blessed with an angelic face and musical talent, he was an asset to Gospel Chapel, the conservative church he grew up in. But Harley was a rebel at heart, reveling in mischief. One Sunday morning while getting dressed for church he stashed a hip flask sized bottle of Jim Beam in his pocket, covering it with a long shirt. Bo, Harley's younger brother noticed the smug gaze he had on his face.

"What are you up to?"

"Nothing," Harley replied as his lips twitched with amusement. Bo, obedient and well behaved, eyed Harley warily during the service. As the organ started to play during the first hymn, Harley disappeared. He went into an empty toilet cubicle and started drinking. He must have been gone twenty minutes because he missed the introductory hymns. When he returned to his seat he was reeking of bourbon and staggering a little.

"Just in time for the sermon," Harley stammered, eyes half closed, while Bo glared at him. When Harley sat down he felt a wet sticky liquid trickle down his thigh.

"Oh shit!" he muttered under his breath, loud enough for Bo to hear. "What have you done now?" Bo chided.

"Give me your jacket," Harley demanded as Bo complied. Harley quickly tied it round his waist, an effort to hide the bourbon stains. No one ever suspected a thing.

Then to his mother's dismay Harley grew his hair long. One time he awoke in the middle of the night with his mother peering down at him, shaking her disapproving head.

"You look disgusting with that hair, an embarrassment to this family," his mother scolded, armed with scissors in hand. With a razor tongue and critical eye it was impossible to please her.

"Jesus had long hair," he snarled then stormed out. Sick of his parents' rigid religious rules he packed his bags at nineteen and hit the road with other musicians. Now in the real world, women and drugs were plenty, partying was nonstop, and his family faded into memory.

Harley read my mind when he suggested we go back to his place. We barely made it to the front door before we were tearing each other's clothes off.

Laying me on the floor, his warm hands closed over my bare thighs. He nibbled and licked my breasts as I groaned with pleasure. My body was on fire. He knew how to tantalize me longing for more. After half an hour of foreplay he invaded me with his strength. Loud moaning filled the room as he brought me to climax over and again.

We lay breathless holding each other. When we regained our strength I felt a new connection, closer to him than ever before. Harley made me a coffee and we hung out for a while.

"Did you hear about the story about the fallen angel?" Harley asked randomly. He often would speak in metaphors, another eccentric trait that lured me in.

"No, how did she become a fallen angel?" I replied.

"The devil seduced her and made her fall in love with him."

"But why would an angel fall for him?" now I was frowning.

"He masqueraded himself as an angel of light."

"There are many wolves in sheep's clothing aren't there?"

"There sure is honey," Harley replied smiling.

An hour later when I announced I was heading home Harley's hands locked onto my hips, grinding his body to mine. He drew in closer kissing me passionately. On the way home I could still feel remnants of the kiss. It felt electric, like fireworks running through me.

Over the following weeks, we were inseparable. I felt an instant affinity with him, convinced I had found my soul mate. His music fascinated me and his scars intrigued me. But never did he let me get close enough to touch them, always keeping a safe distance. When Harley didn't have a swarm of women circling him at Gypsy's, he would usually be sitting on his own in the corner of the room looking wounded and lonely.

When I questioned him about where the relationship was going sometimes and he would vaguely murmur "The answer's blowing in the wind." He seemed so carefree and easy going.

"Ok cool. We will just see where the road takes us," I replied ignoring the knot in my stomach.

We had been seeing each other for a year when Harley told me he had to move out of his place immediately.

"I have nowhere to go, so I'm crashing in my car," he lamented.

I offered to let him to stay with me but he declined saying he didn't want to be a load on my space. He lived in his car for a few months until he received a call from the real estate agency with news of available housing.

I hugged and kissed Harley tightly, laughing when I heard the good news.

"Once I pay the bond I can move straight in, but I need some cash. I'm getting more gigs soon so I can pay you back then."

"How much do you need cuz I don't want to be a walking ATM?" I asked.

"Two grand, I know it's a lot babe but you know I'll pay you back."

"Whoa that's too much. I can only lend you $500." I was struggling to launch my screen printing business but my compassion for Harley and desire to move our relationship took over.

"If I don't pay all of it I will lose the place." I didn't want that to happen after all the time he had spent looking but he had put me in an awkward position.

"You're not manipulating me are you?" I thought if I asked him directly I would know whether he was lying or not.

"No, it's women who manipulated me. The only thing they'd let me do is my music. But you're not like them, you're cool. You get me."

His words sedated me, overriding my doubts. He leaned over, looking deeply into my eyes and kissed me tenderly, caressing my face. I believed God had put me in Harley's path to save him and even join him briefly in the darkness to bring him back to the light. How could I turn him down in this desperate time of need?

Weeks passed without hearing from him and I could not shake my anxiety over lending him the money. Word on the street was a couple of his friends had already seen the place although he promised I would be the first.

I rang him several times to demand answers but he never picked up the phone; he had vanished like a phantom. I pictured him rubbing his hands like a pawn broker, smirking so broadly that his cold eyes narrowed to slits. Days and nights spilled together. I rolled my head on the pillow, unraveling a thin web of sleep from my sore skull. Sharp pains pierced my brain like a knife.

Who was this man that had declared his love to me, had it all been a facade, a trap for me to surrender my money? My brain scrambled to find a logical excuse. Harley saw me as his target not his lover. A trip on his Harley was not the only ride he had taken me on. Harley stole my money, but more precious than that, my innocence, the part of me that longed to soothe his wounds while neglecting my own.

On the walk home I let the pain and anguish wash over me. At first the tears wouldn't come, it was just a numb distant feeling of betrayal. My palms were cold and I was shivering. I turned my face away from the wind, inhaled the cool air into my lungs and breathed out. I meditated to the sound of my heart beating, which stilled my thoughts. I realized my compassion had blinded me, even when my gut was screaming get the hell out of there. Next time, I promised myself I would listen more closely.

I LOST MYSELF TODAY

by Oceania Chase

I thought,
That I'd got past this.

I thought,
That I understood:

That, I'm never right,

Always wrong

That I have no life,
No privacy,
No right to my own future

My destiny is not mine to control
But hers to shape as she sees fit

How dare I have an opinion of my own?
I am but an extension of her ego

What I think,
Is wrong

What I do,
Is wrong

What I say,
Is wrong

No matter where I go,
Or how far I run

Her voice remains in my head
Insistent and strong

You're selfish!

You don't understand!

I did it all for you.
You owe me!

Haven't I paid enough?
When will it end?

Will her death bring peace?
Or just more pain?

For in her death I have no chance
No chance to hear her say...

"I'm sorry"

"I was wrong"

"You were right."

"You did have the right to life,
To live,
To love,
To breathe"

She denies everything – She should take responsibility.

She violates my boundaries – She should have taught me to keep myself safe

She makes favourites out of my siblings, my friends – She should have taught me how to share

She undermines me – She should have built me up

She demeans, criticizes and denigrates me – She should have supported me

She makes me look crazy – There is nothing wrong with me

She envies me – She should have been proud

She lies – At least, in this, she taught me about truth

She must be the centre of attention at all times – How dare I be sick? Even that becomes about her

She manipulates my emotions in order to feed on my pain – I learn to feel nothing so that I feel no pain

She's selfish and willful – I have no right to tell her "no'" She's self-absorbed – My needs are insignificant

She is insanely defensive and is extremely sensitive to criticism – I must be wrong

She terrorizes – I placate at all times

She's infantile and petty – She should have taught me how to grow

She's aggressive and shameless – She doesn't ask, she demands and I obey

She parentifies – At least I learned responsibility

She's exploitive – She should have taught me honour

She projects – But I am not her

She is never wrong about anything – She should have demonstrated remorse

She seems to have no awareness that other people even have feelings – I only broke one bone, not two

She blames – I am at fault

She destroys my relationships – she should have taught me how to relate

As a last resort she is pathetic – In this she is true, she is pathetic

I know all this

I've studied,

I've learned

I understand
She is a narcissist
This mother of mine

She, is the crazy one
She, is the one that is insane

I thought that I'd got past this
I thought,
That I understood:

That, I am right,
Not always wrong

That I have a right to life,
To privacy,
A right to my own future

My destiny is mine to control
Not hers to shape as she sees fit

But today, I dared to have an opinion of my own
I stepped outside of being but an extension of her ego

And instantly, her voice was in my head
Insistent and strong

I do not exist as anything but an imperfect reflection of her

I lost myself today.

FOR SO LONG I AM NOT "ME"

by Ayesha Fayyaz

For so long
I refrained my heart to be pain-stained
I avoided crawling agony
I blocked failure
I wanted to be unbreakable
I was so timid to put my toes in a tub of mistakes
I caged my wild heart in a barbed wire
In all that I let it bled terribly
I felt exhausted deep in my bones
Every cell in my body roared
Like a churning volcano
It took so much energy to pretend.

BY THEN

by Shay Cook

By then the poem
stays inside the
pen and the petals
fall from the rose
and your kisses are
not as sweet and
your touch has
made me cringe
and our love
has turned to soot
and I am glad
you're not under
foot by then.

REALIZATION

by Kelly Baker

You dug your claws in
and got a hold,
as my naivety
you slowly stole.
You crashed my thoughts
of love and peace,
as you weren't close
to giving release.
You made my innocence
bleed...
You decided the cold, hard truth
is what I need.
You let my tears fall,
as you didn't once try to dry my eyes.
You laughed louder
than my screaming cries.
You held me down,
you twisted my arm.
You fooled me
with that fake charm.
That was then,
this is now.
I awoke
and pulled through somehow.
Now as you stand alone
with your misery and defeat,
you realize like a cat,
I always land on my feet.

BULLET, DEMON, SPECTER

by Jo Rider

My eyes are open
but I'm not seeing

My lungs expand
but I'm not breathing

I am alive
but I'm not living

My demons are screaming for blood
Mine, theirs, anyone's, really
It's a funny thing, inner darkness
You'd think you could see it on the outside
A lack of laughter
An absence of a smile
Crying, shouting

The people who seemed depressed
are the ones who probably aren't
While the ones you think are fine
Are simply experts at hiding their pain
Knowing they'd be mocked for weakness, or for seeking attention

When really all they want is a reason to keep living
I'm trapped in a cycle of vengeance and aggression
I'm clinging to a cliff by my fingers
Swept with wind and rain
A part of me wishes to fall
How can I find the strength to climb?

More than that
what path do I pick
what handholds do I grab to pull me to the top?

Which ones will fail me?
Which ones will hold?

I'm scared
but I'm not crying
I'm angry
but I'm not screaming

At least not that anyone but me can hear
I cannot bear it
To be unheard
To be alone
It is a curse.

I would fight back,
I would destroy the walls that deafen my enemies' ears to me
Yet in my proverbial bullet's path
stand those I love

My enemy holds them close with candy
and a grinning specter's smile

The smile of one who is drowning in their own death
and clings to what might keep them afloat
regardless of the harm done to those
they once swore to love

The monsters under my bed
have moved into my head

The beast I thought would eat me in my sleep
is killing me slowly in the day

If dark times are the price for light
then karma may favor me
but I'm not sure I can afford it

The demons in my head
beg me for my blood
my heart

my body
as if my mind weren't enough

I am my own specter
as much as anyone else is
My own greatest enemy
is the one between my eyes

I'm scared
but I cry only when no one can see my tears
I'm angry
and I only scream inside my head
I'm lonely
but I hold no blame to those around me

for who would want me
my bullet
and my grinning specter?

GRAY MATTER

by Jolene Hughes

Life happened. He happened. One thing after another after another after another. I sat and coped. I survived. I retreated to my padded cell within a cave within a gilded box at the center of an impenetrable maze. I stopped writing to deal with the happenings, and the gray matter grew a sick sort of slime mold, the kind that feeds on words and thoughts and feelings, until I had none of those things anymore.

Writing had been a protective force, connected to and strengthened by my soul. The less time spent writing and creating made way for the creeping destruction of my core self, that demolished a piece of my soul's architecture, a room, cross beam, and story at a time. Until I woke realizing I was killing myself by coping. My safe cell had become my prison, and my soul was slowly dying. I could no longer write. It took a year of hard weightlifting, teaching my clumsy hands to draw, and forcing my moldy brain to make my fallow flesh and mind cooperate. I could only draw without thinking about what I was drawing. Then I graduated to painting. Each brush stroke was effort, to the point of tears. Soul therapy is hard work.

Once I could write it felt like a dam broke, vomiting murky water and detritus from a lake's cold trenches over jagged edges and exposing the darkest depths to the glaring scrutiny of a winter sun. The violent shaking split the concrete wall first down the midline, which begat more cracks splitting open, wider, deeper along the curving face of the reservoir. Years of layered sediment, stuffed down by gravity and pressure far from the light and passers-by, and years of ignored hairline fractures led to that moment, those few slow seconds in which a fortress was leveled.

And once I was alive again, I was what happened to him.

Endings

"What's gone and what's past help
Should be past grief."

Shakespeare, *The Winter's Tale*

EMBRACE

by Rehana Campbell

I keep trying to resist,
I keep trying to hold the pieces together.
Each one carelessly glued on,
How am I supposed to attend to them all?
I've been riding the train of optimism for far too long,
And my body can feel it.
It needs a break from feeling whole,
It needs a rest from being strong,
But I'm holding on for dear life.
A fear so familiar it tastes like me,
A fear so insidious it's been there all along,
Underlining my movements,
Magnifying my judgments.
It is not until I tune into the waves and nuances that I finally find compassion,
A meeting of love and pain,
A uniting of loss and empathy.
This is my home, this is my temple,
And I am here to listen to you, my dear.

PERFECTLY DONE

by Sarah Miner

I made his favorite meal the day I filed for divorce. Breaded fish and pasta with butter. I didn't even poison it.

His family's recipe calls for petrale sole, but I used red snapper because it reminds me of childhood dinners in coastal California. And olive oil instead of butter because three-fifths of our family members have a dairy allergy. I can't seem to follow a recipe anyway. Some part of me chaffs at the conformity of making the same thing the same way every time.

I put rolled oats and tapioca flour in the brand new stainless steel food processor he told me to buy for myself. He saw me using it shortly after it arrived on our doorstep in its Amazon Prime box, and commented that he liked making me happy. As if, after everything, a kitchen appliance would be the magic trick to make me happy and forget and forgive so he could be happy.

I pulverized the oats to dust, to more finely coat the fish. Organic dried herbs, a 21-ingredient seasoning blend, went into the flour mix. And salt. He loves salt.

The fish was first dunked in a whisked duck egg from our daughter's flock, then coated on both sides of each fillet with gluten-free breading. Then into the organic olive oil puddle on unbleached parchment paper.

Perfection is important to him. So, dinner was going to be perfect. Finely grated Asiago cheese, his favorite, was on the table. I had skinned my thumb on the stainless-steel teeth. Morbidly I pondered the idea that it was karma that I shouldn't escape this day unscathed, and his karma that I should bleed into the cheese he loved.

I pushed the stoneware laden with glorious snapper into the oven and sat down with my laptop at the dining room table until it was time to start the pasta. He joined me, claiming the chair opposite and pinning me with a stare. Waiting for me to give him his due of my full respect and attention.

"Not to rush you," he said with a tone of voice evidencing his impatience, "but how long are you going to make me wait?"

"Wait for what?" I replied.

"You know what."

I sighed and went back to the kitchen, buying time for my racing pulse and thoughts to return to somewhere near normal.
The spaghetti went into the stainless-steel stock pot, and I set the timer on my phone for nine minutes.

Back at the table and properly in my seat to give him my undivided attention, I returned his stare with an unexpected calmness, a state of which I hadn't felt in years of living in Jekyll and Hyde land. It grounded me with truth and certainty and integrity.

"I'm done," I began, and then explained why I had filed for divorce that morning, or, rather, my lawyer had.

Our marriage was over with two minutes to spare.

He was in shock. He never thought in a million years I'd leave him. He was wrong. Later, in one of the inevitable conversations about why I had written such awful things about him in the divorce petition, I corrected his complaint that I had stabbed him in the back. Rather, I held up a mirror of truth. If he didn't like what he saw there, he shouldn't have made those choices.

He was sorry. And sorry. "Why can't you just forgive and forget?" he asked.

In the two years leading up to that night, I had learned a few things. I had nourished myself on a steady diet of feminism and strength training and art. The problem with forgiving and forgetting is that it is a way of invalidating the victim's experience. It invites "gas lighting." I couldn't truly heal if I worked on forgiving and forgetting. I had to separate the two like squabbling teenaged daughters and deal with each separately.

Forgiving wasn't for him: the person who did the damage and whose footsteps on hardwood floors make me panic. It was for me to heal myself. Forgiveness is a process, not an instant smile-and-be-nice-now button we get to push.

Choosing to forget how I was wounded by him was to deny that he hurt me with lies and betrayal and narcissism and abuse. To forgive and forget is to sip toxic soup. Forgive and remember, on the other hand, that's how to heal. It's harder. And messier. It is soul-work: homework to clear my heart free of scars and darkness.

"Why?" He whined like a petulant child who was reluctant to give up a toy.

"Because I'm the lighthouse. And you didn't change course. For years. And now these are the cliffs."

He rose from the dining room table, escaping to the bedroom to brood in solitude. The children rushed upstairs, as if on cue, and set the table: three eager helpers whose mouths were literally watering at the fragrance from the oven. They hurried through their task and waited in the doorway to carry the food to the table. They hadn't heard our conversation.

The timer buzzed for the pasta. I tossed it in a serving bowl that had been a wedding gift. The sizzling fish went from the oven to a matching platter, was drizzled with lemon juice, and then was arranged for aesthetic value and to prevent the crust from getting soggy.

Chilled white wine was on the menu instead of the usual red. Probably he'd say it was the wrong kind of wine to pair with breaded snapper, but I no longer gave a fuck. It was wine I liked, for once. I knew he'd drink bottles of whatever wine was in the house anyway.

But he walked past the elegant table and the perfect meal and left the house without eating a single bite.

Then I noticed the children had only set the table for four instead of five.

SIBLINGS IN SORROW

by Rehana Campbell

There's a fuzziness that surrounds him I can't describe.
It makes me feel nostalgic,
As if I've missed something he already was.
How are we so in sync,
Yet still so distant in our paths?
A brother oh so loving,
He'd fight wars to uncage me.
Earliest to fly I saw his wings flutter,
Freedom sprung from them as mine began to clutter.
He inspired, I began to comprehend what had happened,
Suddenly I was also flying free from the prison.

Now I sail solo synchronizing my strengths,
But I peer next door to my brother's eyes I'm entrenched.
A love born from sorrow, such no one could ever imagine,
I don't expect you to understand such a contraption.

THE TERRORIST IN MY BED

by Anonymous

It was him or me.

I was not going to die today. And certainly, not at the hands of this mad man, the monster my fiancé had become.

He threw me on the bed while I was holding our 8-week-old baby and began to suffocate me with his hands over my mouth as I struggled to breathe. I saw the demonic look in his eyes. He wanted to kill me. NOW, my mind screamed. Fight back, NOW. I began shaking and kicking to get him off of me, hyperconscious of my baby still being held in my arms, terrified that my child would be hurt during this. As he continued to hold me down, I bit him. Really hard. Feeling like my life depended on that one move, my bite was so vicious that it immediately drew blood. He looked shocked that I fought back and screamed, "You bitch," moving just enough that I could break free. Keeping my tight grip on our child's tiny body, I ran and locked us in the bedroom.

That day began the nightmare. The descent into a dark, secretive, isolating, terrifying world of violence and mental illness. I watched a man with a master's degrees, who once made over six figures at an advertising company, wave a knife around in the kitchen threatening to stab himself and then swallowing an entire bottle of anti-psychotic pills. I had to page psychiatrists at 2a.m. to tell them that he was trying to kill himself. I was shoved, grabbed, pushed, had my hair pulled and was told he wished I was dead and that he was going to kill me. I saw a man, once charming and in control, morph into a man who was erratic, angry, and dangerous; a shell of his former self.

I watched my fiancé cascade down into the dark world of disorder: bipolar, post-traumatic stress, narcissistic personality. I was always plotting my escape. Every day.

I did get out one beautiful, sunny spring morning with my family and the movers waiting in the car. That day I knew I had "crossed" over, but I still never felt like I could breathe a sigh of relief. He was always out there...somewhere. There was the time, after I left, where he told me "don't think I won't hesitate to come over there and kill you, bitch" and I found myself printing out an application to purchase a gun, something I don't even morally believe in, but started to feel might be necessary.

Trying to calculate what window he would smash if he broke into my home, I installed an alarm for the whole apartment. I had a GPS tracker in my child's backpack.

As the weeks, months, and years went on, I began to stand up to him more. There was that pivotal moment where I yelled "Your reign of terror is OVER," feeling liberated and fearful at the same time, but all I could do was just keep going, keep trying to put as much time and distance between the present and the days when we were together, the days when I hid in that bedroom.

But no matter how much time goes by, no matter how much my life changed, I never fully forget. Every time we must interact, I am still overcome by that feeling. What it felt like that day years ago, when I saw that demonic look in his eyes.

That day when I saw him look intent on killing me.

A version of this essay was first published on sammichespsychmeds.com at http://www.sammichespsychmeds.com/?s=the+terrorist+in+my+bed

YOU

by Kelly Baker

I saw secrets hidden beneath your eyes
and being tortured under your lips.
Still, you managed to hold your head high
and leave the door open after you left,
you misled coward!
You condemned me for washing the sheets,
as your eyes shot across the sky.
I could only imagine
how simple you must be,
you unfortunate soul!
I didn't shed a tear
as you fired bullets into my chest
and you questioned my sarcastic smile,
as you told me you love me best,
you washed up fool!
You thought you saw a trembling child,
nothing needed to be tamed.
Now as I stand over this pool of blood,
you must know you're not to blame,
you dead soul!

GHOST SELVES, A LOVE STORY

by Kathryn Peterson

The day I met my now ex-husband, there was snow on the ground. It was early April, but in Cincinnati that year, the weather didn't know it. The snow fell slanted, in uneven drifts, so high it covered the window. I was looking at it from inside, through the steam that obscured the glass. I'd just been accepted into the University of Houston's fiction writing program, and I was excitedly talking on the phone. The woman at the other end was the receptionist at the Baptist Student Center in Houston, because, for some reason, I felt it important to find out what programs they had for graduate students four months before I got there.

I'm not actually sure why I was so adamant to find out about all that. But if I hadn't, I would never have met Scott. When I asked what programs were available for graduate students, the receptionist shrank a little. "Well, we don't offer anything per se," she said. "But we do have graduate students. In fact, one's sitting right here. Let me let you talk to him."

She put me on the phone with Scott. I immediately liked him. He was clearly intelligent, seemed to be very conscious about his spiritual life, and had a quick wit about him. He could turn phrases sarcastically in a way that always used to turn me on. He was suddenly, even in that first conversation, Benedick to my Beatrice, Cheers' Sam to my Diane.

"So your last name is Paterson?" I asked, to which he replied that it was.

"That's so funny," I laughed. "Mine is Peterson."

"Ha ha," he said. "If you married me you would hardly have to change your name."

He'd mentioned he had a girlfriend, but of course I wasn't thinking about anything like that. I knew his comment was a joke. And yet even then it took me aback. I didn't know why then, but now I realize how inappropriate, or at the very least, strange, it was that his mind went there right away. That he would make that comment to a woman on the other end of a telephone line who was nothing more than a perfect stranger.

I see myself now from the outside of that Cincinnati window, my eyes wide in my narrow face. I was pale, slightly overweight, but buxom, blonde and pretty. I was hopeful. And I had no idea what I was about to get myself into.

In retrospect, I was the perfect narcissist target. I was smart and accomplished but also a hopeless romantic and incredibly naive. Because I had not dated anyone for longer than three months, I didn't know what it was like to be in a real relationship. All I knew was that, as a young conservative Christian woman, I was supposed to be careful with men and not allow them to seduce me. The church did a great job of keeping men out of my pants. It didn't do such a good job of keeping them out of my heart.

For some women who marry narcissists, the love bombing happens at the beginning of the relationship. The irony is that in my case, that phase began before Scott and I even officially met. From the moment of that phone call until I arrived in Houston that August, we had what I thought was a close long-distance friendship, but what I now see was the early days of becoming enmeshed. Email was in its early days then, but we were both tech savvy, particularly Scott, who is a computer programmer. He emailed me at least once a week, sometimes every other day; long, beautiful emails. I wish I still had them. If I did, I'd compare them to the ones he'd write later to the woman he courted when he left our marriage.

There was even a point where my Teaching Assistant funding was tenuous and I thought I might put off my admission to graduate school, and it was Scott who talked me into coming. "I'm sure you'll find a way to support yourself," he said one day over the phone. "This is your dream, Kathryn; you have to pursue it."

One day, when I was feeling particularly low, I received a package in the mail. It was a care package, filled with little gifts and small stuffed animals, pencils that had the University of Houston name and logo on them, and a University of Houston mug.

"That guy sent me this." I showed a friend. She was a little concerned. "He has a girlfriend," I said, and shrugged.

"He's after you," one of my guy friends said.

"Well, I'm not interested in him," I said. Which was true. I wasn't really interested in Scott romantically at that point. I just thought he was a sweet friend.

It's funny; even though our relationship lasted eighteen years, the pattern was eerily similar to his with the woman he left our marriage for.

He befriended me the way he would later befriend her, writing long, detailed emails. I wonder if he treated his girlfriend at the time the way he treated me at the end of the marriage -- essentially playing me against the new "friend" and showing me how much I came up short. I never thought about it when we were becoming friends back then, how much the friendship may have threatened the girlfriend. And I never questioned why, when I finally got to Houston, she was suddenly out of his life.

Now, as I sit here, twenty years to the day from when I met Scott in person and two years to the day from when my marriage ended, I finally realize. No man has ever truly loved me. What I thought was love from Scott was really ideation, the same ideation he would later give to the new woman. Scott was my first real love, my first physical relationship, my first relationship of any kind that lasted longer than three months. I thought he loved me, but now, looking back, I see his confusion. I see why, when I broke up with him in November of that same year, it interrupted his ideation-devaluation-discard cycle, and why he was so happy to get back together with me when I changed my mind. Then he broke up with me the following February, and that began what would become five years of a roller-coaster courtship that then ended up, strangely, in marriage.

"I just can't imagine you not in my life," he'd say every time we broke up, no matter which of us was the initiator. "I know, I know," I'd say, and with toxic tears and hoovering hugs, we'd get right back together. To be honest, I think by the time we got married, we were both exhausted. I think we both thought, somehow, that the rings would make the difference. That the toxic cycle we'd become enmeshed in would end and we could "settle" into a peaceful marriage. And truly, the few good times we had were early on in the marriage, when I think we both felt secure enough to approach what might seem close to love.

But the reality is that I don't think it ever was. I think Scott went through cycles of ideation and devaluation and a sort of metaphoric discard even though we could no longer actually discard each other. Like rubber bands, we'd pull back as far as we could from each other before we'd finally snap back together. It was more than just dysfunctional. It was a codependent nightmare.

I didn't see it, though. I'm still not sure whether or not he did. I don't know how much of his mask was conscious and how much was not conscious. I am finally making peace with the fact that I will never know.

"I'm so glad I married you," he'd whisper, taking both my hands. He'd pull me against him and hug me tight, or sometimes lightly kiss me on the lips. "I'm so glad I married you." But was he?

I think this is what sets marriages with narcissists apart from marriages that fail in other ways. When some partners say things like "I don't think I ever loved you," they are rewriting history. When our narcissistic partners say those things, they're telling the truth.

People say no time in a relationship is wasted. That we learn and grow with every person we know and particularly from our mistakes. While the latter may be true, I'm not sure about the former. I grieve the years I lost to my relationship, wonder what would have happened if I'd stayed broken up with Scott that first November, what would have happened if we'd not met in person that day in August, if he'd not been there that day in March to take that first phone call. I certainly wonder what would have happened if I'd never married him. What would I have done? Would I have gone to a different PhD program? Would I now be firmly entrenched in a tenure track job? What would it have been like to be with someone normal? What would it have been like if I had actually been loved? The reality is, of course, that I'll never know. Those ghost selves exist in their alternative timelines, hopefully happier than the one I have now. They float, linger, in the shadows of Scott's own alternate selves, the alternate realities he created. It's all too ephemeral sometimes. Ephemeral, intangible and too damn liminal. But in the end I have to let them go.

I can't redo the past. I can't go back in time and tell that twenty-four- year old in 1996 to watch out, that when the receptionist of the Baptist Student Union hands her the phone, she should run. I can't tell her that, and even if I could, I'm not sure I'd want to. Because even through the hell that has been the end and aftermath of my marriage, I've grown. I've grown in ways I never thought I would and become stronger than I never thought I could be. I think if I were to go back now, I'd just stand, the ghost of me now, beside that young woman.

I would wrap my shadow self around her and I would tell her that I love her, and that I'll be with her, no matter what she must endure. I'll be there when he lets the picture of the ex-girlfriend fall out of his wallet. I'll be there when she cries because he still has the picture and still keeps a portrait of her beside the bed. I'll be there when he says "why are you crying? Because you think she's prettier than you?" I'll be there when he says "Everyone needs a little fat in their diet," and winks and adds "even you." I'll be there when he criticizes her writing and says it reveals a "moral flaw" in her character. I'll be there when he picks out her wedding dress and when he crashes her bachelorette party. When everyone else thinks it's a little weird but sort of cute that she and he are "so close," I'll be there, knowing these are some of the first signs of deeper control.

I'll even be there when it all finally breaks down completely, when he sends that final email, entitled "Kimberly," and that when he decides to leave her for Kimberly, I'll stand there and cheer. I'll whisper in my forty-two year old self's ear "don't fight this; this is your way out. It hurts like hell now but wait, just wait." My forty-two year old self won't believe me, but I'll keep whispering it anyway. I'll whisper it every day and every night until she finally leaves. And when he picks up the cat and flings him across the bed and she sees, finally sees, what he either has always been or has become, I'll put my solid arms around her and wrap her tightly in my own love.

THE LOOKING GLASS

by Rehana Campbell

Looking inwards I see a bulb of liquid,
it moves and jiggles yet stands still.
It isn't like a movie in how it plays,
but it is a story nevertheless, a twisted one.
It is the perspective of my abusers,
those who took my canvas and painted it in a slant.
Everything in this glassy haze is twisted and deformed,
barely completing one another in form.
It is quite unusual to be on this side,
the outside.
It has been a journey,
one of conditioning and one of glory.
However,
the slanted glass is not my mirror,
I am my own soul reflection,
projecting pent up redemption.
I am my own soul redemption,
projecting pent up reflection.

MINDING MOTHER

by Catherine Wald

Take the flimsy paper
doll of your selfhood
wrap it in tissue paper
slip it in an envelope
and mail it to your-
self.

Now you're ready to face
down the headwind
that blows your mother
off course.
Trim her mind's sails,
steer her to calm waters,
keep your hand on the tiller,
don't look back.

At journey's end, she will
set you an enchanted table:
nonsensical nuggets, trivial
tidbits, lurid longings: You

must secretly refuse her.
With your fork, dissect
the quivering aspic of
her memory, stir the
dregs of malice,
watch regrets swirl,
trace etchings on her goblet
with your fingertip but
for God's sake, don't
eat or drink.

You
can do this:

Butterfly into the
net of her need
flit about industriously
and escape
intact
free.

WHEN CARS CRASH

by Erin Laing

Accidents happen. With so many cars on the road, each driver aggressively driving defensively, car crashes are inevitable. More times than not, you're in the wrong place at the wrong time. Other times, you knowingly get into a car with a reckless driver or convince yourself a careless driver will pay attention, just this one time. I'm not sure which is the most upsetting kind of mishap. I'm not sure which type of accident I have been in.

When we crashed, it wasn't clear how bad the collision had been. It's hard to gauge these things when you're still inside the wreckage. I kept thinking we lost a hubcap or dented the fender. It didn't feel like the car was in ruins.

"Are you okay?" he asked, as he tenderly wiped a bit of blood from my cheek.

"I told you we were heading towards a wall," I said resentfully. That's when I noticed everything was upside down. I was getting dizzy from the blood rushing to my head.

"I know," he said confidently. He undid my seatbelt and gently pulled me out from the debris. I didn't understand how he got out before me, completely unscathed.

"So why did you hit it?" I smelled smoke.

"Because the sun was in my eyes." He took a long pause. "Besides, I need to know what it feels like to fall in love again."

Boom! The car went up in flames.

"At my expense?" I said, mesmerized by the sparks.

"I saved you, didn't I?"

All I could do was laugh. Apparently, it's a normal reaction when your body experiences trauma. As Oscar Wilde once said, "life is too important to be taken seriously." So, I laughed. A lot.

I laughed as I remembered him dancing the nights of his birthdays away, with every woman except me. I laughed when I remembered him telling me that I didn't live up to his expectations of who he thought I could be. Hysterical, I told myself, as I watched the car incinerate.
"What's so funny?" he said.
I was laughing so hard I couldn't speak.

"What's so funny?"

"I don't have insurance," I said, in a bout of hysterics.

"It was worthless anyway," he said, encouragingly.

Would you like more fuel to add to the fire? I thought. "It wasn't worthless to me." I stood up, my legs still shaking.

"Where are you going?" he asked nervously.

"Away."

"How long will you be gone?" There was a tone of regret in his voice. "I don't know." I began to walk away.

"Will you send me a postcard?" he asked, like a bewildered child.

"Sure," I said, not thinking straight.

"I can't wait to see how you represent me in your work," I could hear him say from a distance. Right, I thought. I was stranded on a deserted Canadian highway, with no mode of transportation, and those were the last words he said to me.

"Narcissism is a disease" were the first words my therapist said to me, six months later, as I sat, haunted by my car crash, in her humble office in Berlin. I paid someone eighty Euros for that advice. But it was good advice.

"Should I have bought insurance?" I asked.

"What difference would it make?"

"It would cover the cost of these sessions." She didn't laugh.

"How long was the drive?" She asked.

I did the math quickly in my head. "2,628,000 kilometers." A sizable distance.

Roughly three years.

"How were the roads?"

"Full of potholes," I said, not skipping a beat. It was true. Communist regimes take better care of their roads than the province of Quebec.

"Why didn't you look for a different course?"

"Because. The scenery on our route was to die for." "Apparently. I'm surprised you didn't crash sooner."

Her sarcasm was not bracing. "Well, I drove occasionally, and I'm a very confident driver," I said. "Besides, I spent most of the time parking. I love parallel parking."

"When did you see the wall?" She asked knowingly.

"Right before we hit it."

I lied. I saw it the first time he opened the car door for me.

"I'm not a very good driver," he said, as I got into the passenger seat.

"I like to go
pretty fast, get as far as I can before I run out of gas."

"You look like a responsible driver."

"I've been in two serious accidents."

I responded naively, distracted by the fresh coat of paint on the car. "I'm sure they weren't your fault."

It was cool in her office but I could feel the backs of my thighs sticking to the leather seat. I kept thinking about all the people before me, sitting across from her and her cream colored wall, talking about their car wrecks. Did they too, rip their cuticles while they spoke? Cross their arms and legs and tap their feet to an inaudible beat?

"Tell me about your parent's car," she asked sympathetically.

"I don't remember it. It crashed when I was ten. My mother drives a Prius, my father, an SUV. To be honest, I hate cars. I hate how we're so dependent on them. I hate what they represent. I much prefer walking or riding my bike."

"Driving has its advantages."

Perhaps, I thought. "There was a long stretch of paved roads." My knee was jerking up and down.

"I'm sure there was."

"Months where the clouds held the sun hostage."

"And?"

"Then the sun broke free." My mind wandered. I was lost in thought. ----

"Where are we going again?" I asked him, spinning the map, round and round in my hands. I was confused as to why we were the only ones on the road.

"Not sure yet."

"I thought you knew where we were going?" I asked with a hint of concern.

"I changed my mind." He was irate. "Just like that, without telling me?"

"Yes."

"Why didn't you say anything?" He didn't answer.

"Can I take over? You seem tired."

"I'm fine."

"Well, do you know how long it will take to get there?"

"I don't know. We'll get there when we get there."

I took a moment. "You've been before, right?"

"Will you stop asking so many questions!" he shouted.

"I just want to know where we're going! Otherwise I'm useless with the map." He took the map from my hands and threw it out the window.

"Wonderful," I muttered.

"We don't need it."

"I needed it."

"So, you won't drive then."

But I love driving, I thought. "You gave me a pretty bad paper cut."

"I'm sorry. I get angry when the sun is in my eyes." He took my hand and kissed my finger.

I wondered if things would have been different had it been a cloudy day.

"No," my therapist said firmly, snapping me back to reality.

"But I'll never know."

"You don't need to know."

"Yeah but..." I saw the look in her eyes. "He only drove poorly when the sun was out." My excuses were gnawing at the bit to be heard.

"Then he should have been wearing sun glasses."

"He didn't own any. Should I have bought him a pair?"

"He would have lost them eventually."

I didn't say it, but she knew what I was thinking.

"You would have wasted a lot of money on sunglasses."

I took a sip of water. "The sun only came out ten percent of the time," I said half jokingly.

"That ten percent almost killed you."

I suppose, I thought. "I hate the sun."

"The sun has nothing to do with it."

I liked that we faced each other. Our relationship felt more like a rowboat. She steered but let me lead the way. She trusted me more than I trusted myself. For a moment, I wondered if there would be fewer accidents if people had to face each other while they drove.

"I was always so tired."

"I can imagine," she said caringly.

"I was always dozing on and off." The recollection made me yawn. She didn't respond. She knew my memory had been triggered.

"Why don't you lie down in the back?" he suggested kindly.

I looked behind us and noticed, for the first time, his entire luggage. "There's a lot of baggage back there. Are we picking anyone else up?"

I asked in jest.

"No. Does it bother you?"

"There's just an awful lot. Do you think we can go through it and get rid of some of it?"

"I need it."

"All of it?"

"It's all I have."

And so, I took a back seat.

I looked at my therapist analyzing strands of her gray hair. It's one thing when the person you love makes you feel invisible. It is something else entirely when the woman you're paying eighty Euros an hour appears jaded by your stories.

"I'm listening," she said, somewhat convincingly.

It was too late. My insecurities had flooded back.

"Don't get too comfortable back there," he said, turning around, several weeks later. I was rubbing residue of rouge from his canvas valise. "I need you to pay attention to the signs," he said.

"I can't see the signs from back here."

"So why don't you sit up front?"

"Because you keep offering my seat to every hitchhiker we pick up."

"That's because they have something interesting to talk about."

You mean like that sign? I thought. I'd get out at the next rest stop except I have no idea where we are. Where I am. "It's easier if I just stay back here."

"You're right. Besides, you look so beautiful in my rear-view mirror." Backhanded compliments always have a way with me.

"Sounds like a charming ride," my therapist said. Her sarcasm was surprisingly refreshing.

It took a couple of weeks but my thighs no longer stuck to the black leather seat. I let the chair embrace my impression.

"Are you angry that you got in the car?" she asked me.

"No." That much I was confident about. I was angry with myself because a part of me wanted to get back into the car. "It's normal."

"No, it's not!"

"Yes. It is," she said reassuringly.

"Why would I have the desire to get back into a car knowing that it's going to crash? Knowing that I could die?"

"Because. You want that rush of adrenaline. It's like any drug." I never pictured myself as an addict of any sort.

She remarked that my legs were still. My arms relaxed.

"I'm ashamed of myself."

"Why?"

"Just because."

"Don't be. We always remember what we've learned."

"I almost died."

"But you didn't die."

"Was I in the wrong place at the wrong time?" I asked, attempting to exculpate myself, one last time.

"What difference does it make?"

"I guess it doesn't."

"Forget about the car. Appreciate the roads you discovered."

"I would have never seen them if it weren't for him."

"So, thank him," she said, almost too enthusiastically. I started to laugh but it was a different kind of laugh.

"What's so funny?"

"Everything and nothing."

She perked her eyebrows and smiled delightedly.

It was so simple. "He didn't want sunglasses. Did he?" I said.

"No. He didn't."

"It's too bad," I said, with pained relief. "He would have worn them well."

"I'd still like to find out about this Prius your mother drives. I'm thinking of buying one."

"Some other time," I said with a confident grin. "I do know she has insurance though."

To which she laughed. "They always do."

They say it helps to return to the scene of the crime to give oneself closure. So, I did. The car was long gone but remnants of our crash remained: a battery from the watch I had bought him for his thirtieth, a half-finished crossword puzzle, the edges burnt. No crime scene would be complete without whispers of our former selves.

"I thought you would thank me," I could hear him saying.

"For what?"

"I saved you, didn't I?"

Damn. He made it into my work.

LIMITLESS

by Rehana Campbell

When you are in the tidal wave,
You can't see it for what it is.
Instead, it is a rush of curling motion,
Sweeping your head sideways,
Scooping your body.
You feel it, you don't see it,
A cartwheeling blur,
Some heavy weight launching you endlessly.
There is a sense of being lost,
A dizziness from the flurry of bubbles perhaps,
Look how present you are being under such a circumstance!
Smiling inward, you sting of motivation and feeling,
A surge of reorientation takes lead.
Hands whip out at either side,
And legs follow lead to find sand solid soles.
Once you were lost, but now you are found,
And lost you will probably find again.
Underneath the sand you see the glimmer,
A bottle containing a script of paper:
"A happy home awaits your return,
You created it when you chose self over harm,
A key to unlocking your limitless world,
You are free to explore the expanse of your soul."

MORE THAN HELP

by Catherine Wald

The voicemail from my mother is in her lost-little-girl voice, the one she uses to let me – the world – know she needs someone to take over, take charge, save her. Help is such a small, harmless-sounding word, so self-contained with its light vowel, soft consonants and spare syllable. What my mother wants, if there was a word for it, should have at least eleven syllables and be written in bold, in all caps.

How did a presumably mature adult come to expect such bounty (if rescue, indeed is, bounty) from the universe? Maybe she took the fairy tales she read to me as a child too seriously, or maybe her mother (a frustrated opera singer) told some fancy tales of her own? Poor Minette, married to a poorly educated furniture merchant, a Russian Jew to her more refined German. Regrets? She had only one. *If only I'd married my lieutenant.*

Mom's legacy: the belief that being the object of attention is infinitely superior to taking care of oneself, that asking for help/approval/ recognition/interest from strangers is far better than growing a sense of confidence, value and self-reliance. To her, the ultimate success is not accomplishing something, but in manipulating someone —anyone— into doing it for her.

I wish I only took after my mother in trivial habits like accosting strangers on the street. I wish that every day I didn't check my voicemail, email, bricks & mortar mailbox expecting that something or somebody is going to come along to CHANGE MY LIFE. I wish every time my husband annoyed me – which is often enough – I didn't find myself muttering my own ridiculous version of *If only I'd married my lieutenant!* I chose him from a place of wholeness, not wistfulness.

I am furious at my mother for choosing to be crippled by despair, for renouncing her God-given autonomy, for setting the bar for her own happiness so incredibly low.

She has always loved the song from Walt Disney's Snow White "Someday, My Prince Will Come." She actually has the sheet music hanging in her apartment. At 82, is she still waiting? I don't dare to ask, and I don't want to be told.

NEEDS

by Terri Elders

"I've got a proposition for you."

Of course, he did. My ginger-haired Charlie Watson always had an offer to make. Would I like to drive to Palm Springs for calamari for lunch? Or read his latest poem and suggest a paying market? Or accompany him to the Forum to root for the Lakers? Or join the Peace Corps and live in some obscure Caribbean country for a few years?

Since I'd always agreed in the past, even before he'd spelled out his latest proposal I suspected I'd assent once again.

So, we perched close together on the seawall near the Baron Bliss Lighthouse monument in Belize City's historic Fort George neighborhood. Charlie slung a freckled arm around my shoulders and proceeded to beseech me to move with him to La Antigua, Guatemala. I'd anticipated this might be his ploy.

We'd each spent some time in that colonial former Guatemalan capital the previous year, studying Spanish. It wasn't hard to be charmed by its cool highland air, cobblestoned streets, art galleries, wine bars, and shops full of tipico garments. I knew Charlie loved the town.

I also knew that he didn't love me. But I knew damned well that he still needed me. For nearly a decade I'd been his off-and-on lover, as well as his companion, champion, cheerleader, critic and editor.

I may have not been strong in the first of these roles, but I sure excelled at the last. No point in false modesty. I've always had a good eye for spotting grammar gremlins, all those misplaced modifiers, dangling participles, and unclear antecedents that muddy a reader's initial perceptions. Don't get me started on the misuse of "due to" and "hopeful." I may not be able to diagram a sentence in the classic style of those halcyon days of yore, but I know the meaning of both "halcyon" and "yore."

I can spot when a semi-colon is called for; even today, my writing partner, a woman twenty years my junior, swears she'd sleep with me herself if, somehow, she could absorb through proximity my sense for where to insert a clarifying comma.

Charlie, though, needed more than a comma-placer. He needed somebody to cry "whoa" when he galloped out of control, piling clunky simile upon awkward metaphor. I'd always tried to rein him in. Sometimes

I succeeded.

For example, who, other than Charlie, would ever dare to write that someone's hair was "bushier than Alley Oop's," felt as if he'd been "cold cocked by Joe Louis," had eyes "sadder than a cocker spaniel" and lounged in a room "so filled with silence he could hear a frog fart"...all in the same paragraph? It might be entertaining, but not in the way Charlie intended. He seriously as a writer wanted to be taken seriously.

Now he spelled out his plan. We'd rent a place together. We'd be housemates. We'd write and rewrite, cook suppers for one another or go out to schmooze with other expats at our favorite bistros. After all, Charlie reminded me, La Antigua featured every international cuisine you could dream of, from Korean to Kosher. We'd continue our relationship in yet another country. This would make the third since we'd first met at the Paradise Café in Long Beach, California all those years ago. Maybe eventually there'd be a fourth or fifth. Costa Rica. Ecuador. Just think of it...we'd be just like Hemingway and Hadley, Scott and Zelda.

Except...we weren't. Unlike those figures from the flapper era, we were neither young nor dashing. And something else was missing...my role. I, too, harbored creative yearnings. I had untold tales and I wanted the opportunity to write them, not spend every minute tending to Charlie's needs. For the moment, I held my tongue.

Charlie continued with his pitch. "I have an idea for a novel about everything that's happened to us here in Belize and more. It'll be different from the twaddle that other Volunteers have scribbled. I'm talking about bona fide fiction. I'll couple Carl Hiassen's ironic approach to action and adventure with the magical realism of all these terrific Latin American authors. It'll be a hybrid, sure, but I know I can pull it off. I even have a title, *The Toughest Job*."

Of course, I recognized the allusion to the Peace Corps motto, "the toughest job you'll ever love."

Charlie squeezed my shoulder. "Listen, I know I can do it. You know it, too. If you'll front the expenses and keep track, I'll eventually pay you back. Every penny. Either when I sell my book, or when I inherit some money from my mother."

He finally fell silent. I looked into his azure eyes and turned away. I gazed out at the sea, considering.

So, in addition to the other roles, I'd have a new one...benefactor.

Well, why not? I had a little nest egg, a Workman's Comp settlement when Charlie and I had been mugged after our Peace Corps swearing-in ceremony. I'd been stabbed, suffered a permanent partial loss of the use of my left arm from a severed brachial artery. Charlie had been hit across the forehead with a fence rail. He'd had plastic surgery to repair the dent, but didn't qualify for any monetary benefits.

I did a quick calculation. Charlie's mom was in her early eighties and had been ailing for the past couple of years. I figured I'd get repaid from his inheritance sooner than I would from his advance or royalties, if he ever got either. Sure, I believed in his talent and imagination. But I also knew Charlie lacked craft, the ability to weave narrative, description, action, and dialogue into a seamless creation. And though I had an eye for detail, I certainly couldn't structure an entire novel. I could only edit and suggest. Charlie often tended to see my suggestions as criticism, and would bristle. He also could lapse into language that would make me cringe. Once I'd edited out "slicker than deer guts on a doorknob" only to have him reinsert it.

But if I didn't agree to Charlie's proposition, what were my options? We'd both escaped our draining jobs with social services agencies in Los Angeles to reinvent ourselves as international adventurers. Did I want to return to Southern California to take up again, in my middle fifties, the same kind of mind-numbing work at another HMO, or in child abuse treatment or substance abuse intervention, that had ground me down in the first place? I couldn't see any alternatives. And if I did go back, it would be without Charlie. He'd made it clear he'd live in La Antigua, with or without me. If I refused, I figured he'd hit up his mom for an advance on that inheritance.

So, here's where I confronted my needs: I couldn't envision living my life without him. I adored him. A psychiatric social worker by training, I'd always been aware that Charlie frequently became hypomanic. I'd watched him go without sleep for three days while he cranked out a grant proposal, and accompanied him on two hundred mile drives to Puerto Nuevo Baja California just to satisfy a craving for a lobster supper. He'd never had delusions or hallucinations, but he often overestimated his capabilities.

Like other effervescent hypomanics, he could be the life of the party.

"I can take over the room," he used to say. But it was this very energy, drive and optimism, this passion for living and for literature that had attracted me to him in the first place. He had great taste in poetry, and was the only man I knew who worshipped both Emily Dickinson and Charles Bukowski. His outgoing personality made him equally at home with the members of the Los Angeles County Board of Supervisors he'd worked for as an aide and with the blind newsstand operator at his apartment complex.

Or he could become irritable and sullen. I'd seen that side, too. "Well?" Charlie patted my hand.

I took a deep breath and leaped into Charlie's dream. "No problem," I said, with a grin. We'd often laughed together at that ubiquitous Caribbean phrase, often soothingly uttered in the face of dire situations. "I can't miss the chance to do a good deed for my best friend."

Charlie hugged me so tight that it reminded me of another of those similes I'd persuaded him to discard. Something, I can't remember what, had been as tight as a soda straw with a knot in it. Oh, come on!
I should have heeded that old saying: if you want trouble... find yourself a redhead. But I didn't. So, we finished our Peace Corps stint, and then leased a cute casita on Quinta Avenida Norte, tucked between the ruins of a colonial church, San José El Viejo, and a coffee finca populated by dozens of tropical birds, including iridescent hummingbirds, known locally as "garden jewels."

The white stucco house combined colonial charm with plate glass modernity. The door off the cobbled street lead directly to a tiny patio garden filled with fuchsias and impatiens. The kitchen and dining area were on the main level, with steps leading up to a vast living room, big as a basketball court, as Charlie used to brag.

Another set of steps led downwards from the dining area to a cool semi-subterranean area with two bedrooms and a bath. I had the room to the left, and Charlie the one to the right. We installed two desks for our word processors. Charlie plopped a futon on the floor of his room, his pallet of choice as long as I'd known him. Not fond of spiders for bedmates, I purchased a double bed, a cama matrimonial.

Even as the furniture store men delivered it, I wondered if we'd ever use it in any matrimonial fashion. Charlie and I hadn't been lovers for a while. I'd said we were "off and on," but where sex was concerned in this complicated relationship of such long duration, it was mostly off. Thinking about that aspect of our friendship made my eyes as sad as Charlie's cocker spaniel.

When it came to me, Charlie was rarely as ready as a rooster at sunrise, as he'd written in one of his earlier sex scenes.

"I'm such a visual guy," he'd once said. "I can't help myself. I like women who are lean and athletic. You're such a sweetheart, but you've put on a few extra pounds, particularly around the middle. Sorry, but that tummy really turns me off."

It hadn't when we first met. In those days, I lived on coffee, white wine, and cigarettes. But when I kicked a 30-year smoking habit, I'd gained 30 pounds. Charlie couldn't cope with my increased girth. Neither could I, really. I'd lost about half of those extra pounds hiking around Belize for two years, but no matter how hard I tried, my post-menopausal metabolism seemed to trump my efforts to shed the rest.

So, there it was. He needed slim, and I needed him. One of us surely would be thwarted.

We soon settled down into our daily routine, Charlie working on the book from 10 to 4, and me writing travel stories for periodicals: Transitions Abroad, International Living, Miami Herald, Costa Rica Times. Small checks trickled in, but once changed into quetzales the money was enough to treat ourselves to a few special suppers out, or even a weekend once in a while in Panajachel or Guatemala City. We took to rekindling the physical side of our relationship on such occasions, engaging in what we called a celebratory cuddle.

Two years along, Charlie had finished a couple of bulky novels and had embarked on yet a third. He'd also embarked on a persistent flirtation with the girlfriend of his best Antigua pal, a German who operated a restaurant and usually was too drunk to notice. Moreover, he found time to write regularly to an old girlfriend in California, repeatedly suggesting she visit with an eye towards eventually retiring to La Antigua. Years earlier he'd shown me some poems he'd written about her. He called her Los Angeles Lily.

Maybe Charlie thought I didn't care, but I did. I'd always laughed at the lyrics of The Main Ingredient's "Everybody Plays the Fool." But now I believed them. No matter how easy it is to talk about open relationships, I began to feel like a victim, a sucker.

What had I been thinking? Despite his insistence that he'd never marry again, I guess I'd wanted to believe Charlie eventually would realize I was too invaluable to abandon, that he depended on me too much to lose me. I'd always thought I'd wear him down, and he'd finally make me one more proposition. In retrospect, maybe I suffered from a little grandiosity myself.

My savings started to dwindle. Charlie had no nibbles from any agents or publishers, and continued to refuse my suggestions for major revisions of his manuscripts. He'd agree to edits for spelling, grammar and usage, basic proofreading and line editing, but when it came to discussing structure, tone, consistency of voice, he'd turn a deaf ear.

"Remember," he'd growl. "I'm the writer here. You're not writing this book."

One morning Charlie announced he'd heard from Los Angeles Lily that she'd arranged to come for a week's holiday. Maybe this would be a good time for me to visit my family and friends in Southern California. Devastated, I agreed.

During that northern hiatus, my son, who'd had my power of attorney during my overseas years, suggested I pay attention to my advancing age and my declining bank account.

"You're only 53, and you've got years to go before you qualify for Social Security. What are you going to do when your savings run out? How will you get a job when you return to the States?"

I had no answers. I'd not ever thought of returning to the States. Not without Charlie.

When I arrived back in La Antigua two weeks later, I found Lily had left a note atop my word processor. "How kind of you to offer your room," she'd written.

In those days, a person didn't need a prescription for many psychotropic medications, so after a week of steady weeping, I dragged myself to Farmacia Fenix and ordered myself a month's supply of Tofranil. After a while I began to think a little more clearly. My depression began to lift.

"I can't continue to support us both for much longer," I notified Charlie.

Charlie looked surprised. "What are you planning to do?"

"I think we could join the Peace Corps again, serve a couple of years more somewhere. Then we'd have our readjustment allowances, several thousand bucks between the two of us, and that could keep us going for a few more years here, if we decide to return."

Charlie hadn't learned much Spanish while we'd live in Guatemala, but I reminded him that Peace Corps works with trainees intensively, and that he'd pick it up if he were immersed, living with a Spanish-speaking family and not just hanging out with expats as he'd been in Guatemala.

He finally agreed. We applied and both were accepted, and offered, as I'd predicted, assignments in the same Spanish-speaking Caribbean country. We started to think ahead.

Then a couple of months before our scheduled departure date, Charlie told me that he'd changed his mind. He wanted to remain in Antigua. He'd learned that his mom would give him an advance on his promised inheritance. He'd buy a house, and devote his time to finishing the third novel, which was set, not unexpectedly, in La Antigua. It would be a spy spoof, he announced. He seemed quite mirthful and totally unaware that my heart nearly had stopped.

"Charlie, there's an alternative. I could sell my condo in California. We could get married, and we could buy a house together here." I held my breath.

He looked aghast. "You know I never plan to marry again. Besides, you're so needy. I can't stand it when you burst into tears or seem so desperate. But you'll still be my sweetheart," he promised. "I'll visit you this Christmas, and you can come back here the following Christmas."

So, I left and he stayed. True to his word, he spent that Christmas with me in my new country, amusing my fellow Volunteers with his wit. Charlie always commanded the room, no doubt about it. But I didn't go there the next Christmas. He'd invited Lily. He asked me to come for Thanksgiving instead.

Charlie proudly showed me his new home, the sundeck he'd built, and his tomato plants. He talked about how I could rent a nearby apartment when I returned in another year. He kissed me goodbye at Aurora airport.

He continued to send me chapters of the new book to edit for a while. Then he wrote that he was putting it aside for a bit. He'd decided to concentrate instead on writing brief hilarious sketches of daily life in Antigua for a local English-language paper. I thought that really was more his genre than the convoluted novels he'd dedicated so much time to. I wrote, congratulating him on this decision to take a break.

Not long after, one day I stopped by my local post office and found two letters from Charlie in my box. In those days before the Internet and email, it took letters a few weeks to travel from La Antigua to the sleepy town where I now lived. In his first letter, he wrote that he'd met an American woman, a psychologist. She was doing some work with orphanages. She'd rented a bedroom from him.

"She cooks a great chicken parmigiana," he wrote. "She makes it with tomatoes fresh from our garden."

I noticed the "our," and opened the second letter, postmarked a week later. He'd asked her to marry him and they'd set the date for the next month. He gushed about her virtues, how she was everything he'd ever dreamed of.

How hypomanic, I decided. But my response, I now realize, was triggered by jealousy and envy. I sent a telegram demanding he repay me the $18,000 I'd laid out over the years we'd "shared expenses."

"Don't have it," he telegraphed back. "Don't worry. You know I'll repay it. Remember our agreement."

I couldn't think of what to do next. I dreaded returning to California, so I transferred to yet another Peace Corps assignment in yet another country. This time I ended up in the middle of the Indian Ocean, the other side of the world. I sold my California condo, and put the money away for what I envisioned would be my lonely old age.

From time to time Charlie dropped me a note. He'd found an agent for his books. A publisher was interested in this one or that. He still had high hopes for all of them. His wife was generous. She'd paid to remodel his kitchen. But she was starting to act depressed and had gained a lot of weight.

Peace Corps closed its office in this new country so I went to work directly for its government. One day I met an American man who liked me, and didn't mind my extra pounds. He had a few extra, as well. He travelled for a company that contracted with United States military bases and installations, and we became lovers. After he left, we kept up a steady correspondence. I wrote to Charlie that I was thinking about soon returning to the States. Wanted to see what might work out there with this new man, who spent his spare hours pouring over the Wall Street Journal and speculating on the stock market, rather than writing unsalable novels.

This man and I met for one delicious honeymoon-like vacation in Singapore. We sat at the Long Bar at Raffles Hotel sipping Singapore Slings and sharing stories of past romantic follies. I told him about Charlie.

"You'll never see one penny of that money you spent supporting him," he said. "You were such a patsy. Besides, haven't you ever heard that redheads are untrustworthy?"

"Come on...I'm not superstitious. And I really believe he'll pay me back. He might want me to do some editing for him again someday."

My new love laughed, and leaned over and gave me a kiss that made my scalp sizzle.

Not long before I left for the States, Charlie wrote that his home in Guatemala had been badly damaged by a flood. He'd separated from his wife, and filed for divorce. The marriage had lasted just fifteen months. Apparently, she'd gained thirty pounds. And those crying babies she kept bringing home from the orphanage had prevented him from concentrating on his fiction. He suspected she might have dissociative identity disorder; she was such a Jekyll and Hyde.

I was not surprised. All the women in Charlie's life he eventually labeled as crazy. I had plentiful good company.

Later, after I'd settled in a city not far from the one Charlie had grown up in, he phoned. He'd been caring for his mother in her final days, and she'd finally succumbed to cancer. Would I like to come and spend a few days with him before he returned to La Antigua? And would I help with any of the old manuscripts? He'd paid a professional literary agency to comment on his second book, one set in the southwest during the '30s, a strange mishmash of a coming-of-age tale that I could never quite get, starring a hard-hearted hussy and an innocent Charlie-like youth.

"The critic says it needs judicious editing," he said.

"You know what? I agree. You need a pro. Somebody you don't know personally, that you won't make cry when you snarl at a well-intended suggestion."

Though I'd refused the ponderous novels, I did agree to look at any short stories or poems he'd care to send. And he did. By then we both had Internet access and we corresponded frequently. Over the years, I gave him some writing advice that he usually ignored as I continued my own way with my own jobs and my own writing. He no longer made me cry. That interim relationship with Mr. Fiscally Astute didn't work out, but my next one did. I married a man of great wit and charm, who had absolutely no desire to write anything longer than an email. Charlie even visited us once or twice. The two men seemed to enjoy one another.

Then Charlie developed some cardiac problems. With a pacemaker, he no longer could tolerate the altitudes of the highlands. He sold his home in Guatemala, and returned to the city of his childhood. We continued to correspond. He still had hopes of marketing one of the novels. But he grew weaker and sicker and his emails grew briefer. I'd sold a few stories and he encouraged me to keep writing. I finally wrote a story about him and his love of basketball as a birthday present. I filed the email he sent in response: "A wonderful birthday present. Thanks ever so much for a story of memories and good times."

The last email I filed from him alluded to a story I'd written about my mother: "Just splendid-- my favorite of your work -- don't stop writing -- you have so much to share." A couple of months after he sent it I got an email from his niece. He'd died and left instructions in his will that my travel expenses to his family memorial service be covered. I went. I reminisced about our days together in Central America and how much I'd hoped he'd publish the first book, the one about the Peace Corps. I took along dozens of snapshots to share with his family.

"Did the two of you ever become more than just friends?" his niece asked, looking at a picture of Charlie and me at Tikal. I burst into tears. Apparently, Charlie still could make me cry.

Eventually I finally retired and moved to the Pacific Northwest with my husband. He, too, died a few years ago, and we held a family memorial service here. We planted a plum tree in his honor. I remain close to his sons and grandkids.

That flame from my Indian Ocean days? He lost a bundle when the market crashed, but managed to regain most of it. He emails and phones from time to time. We're elderly now, so we prattle about grandkids rather than grand passions.

I spend my days writing narrative essays for feel-good anthologies, and editing books and manuals. It helps me meet my mortgage payments, since my Social Security payments are modest, given all my years overseas as a Volunteer. Books with my bylined stories fill an entire shelf now.

Oh, by the way. When I visited him after his mom died, Charlie handed me a check for $18,000. I immediately put it into a Certificate of Deposit, on the advice of Mr. Stocks and Bonds. Just last fall I cashed in that old CD to purchase a Nissan Altima.

I've never believed the bromide that no good deed goes unpunished. I'm more inclined to think what goes around comes around. So, each time I settle behind the wheel of my new vehicle, I thank Charlie Watson for buying me such a nice car. I really needed one.

Originally published in 2013 in *Loving for Crumbs*, edited by Jonna Ivins.

LOVE NEVER HAD ANYTHING TO DO WITH HER ANYWAY

by Linda Maxwell

She considered . . . while playing solitaire
That the reason the fiancé chose Vicki
And the husband chose Mella
Was not because of the handful of flab
That she couldn't suck in
Or the curls she couldn't control
Or the toenails that grew too quickly.

She realized . . . while finishing the popcorn
That the reason the second boyfriend chose his ego
And the second husband chose his arrogance
Was not because of the breasts she lacked
Or the fortune she wished she had
Or the wit that was Wilde's alone.

She decided . . . while writing the essay
That it wasn't the things she did
Like leaving her shoes by the door
Or laundry drying on the exer-cycle
That turned off the faucet of their love.

She knew . . . while deleting Match.com
That neither was it the things she didn't do
Like marinating gourmet meals at midnight
Or looking Mary Kay mesmerizing in the morning
Or booking the honeymoon suite through Monday
Or mending the socks.

It was all the little boys' search for love that left her alone
With a single blank page.
It was the children's ideal that led them
To find an approving voice like mom's.

A squeezed checkered dishcloth flattened on the sink

A broom always ready in the corner
A dish of dry orange slices on the end table.
To comfort him as his mother had
That stranger that he pushed away
To become the complicated man
He thought all women wanted.

So love never had anything to do with her anyway
That's why she gave it
Away.

THE FOREST FOR THE TREES

by Chauna Craig

Some trees were already dead the year before I left my husband. Others were dying. The mountainside above the Smith River, once a forest lush with lodgepole and ponderosa pine, surrendered slowly, giving up the green with patches of rust then brown then the ashy gray of memorial spires. The very name, evergreen, unraveled to its core lie.

"Beetles," said the neighbor who'd once worked for The Department of Montana Fish & Wildlife and owned the cabin beside ours. "Beetles the size of a grain of rice are doing all that."

There are over a hundred species of bark beetles in the United States. Fewer than one percent of those attack and reproduce in living trees. The mountain pine beetle, culprit of the forests of western Montana, is one of the rare aggressive types, its highly-sophisticated chemoreceptors designed to identify host trees and assess the potential for a successful invasion before even tasting the bark.

The trees in the forest overlooking the Smith River had been under threat long before any visible changes.

The initial attacks are usually limited to the weakest trees: those damaged by fire or root disease, those overcrowded or simply past their healthy prime. The beetles lay their eggs under the bark. Normally the tree's pitch flow kills invaders, but these beetles introduce a blue stain fungus that blocks the flow. The eggs can't be flushed out, and nutrients can't travel up to the branches and needles. Between the fungus and the hungry larvae, the tree is effectively girdled. Slowly, within a year or more, the infested tree dies, its needles reddening, graying, then dropping.

Nearly a year had passed since our last vacation. In the summer of 2009 we stared from the canyon walls to the forested mountainside, trying to remember the previous summer. How many trees had been dying then? Why hadn't we noticed? I'd spent all the summers of my childhood at that cabin, and while the meadow had nearly always been drought-yellow, I remembered only greenest forest. Now red and gray peppered the view, reminding me of a photo I'd once accidentally sprayed with a fine mist of water. The image dissolved, starting with the tiniest holes that bled into one another until the picture was ruined. What would this place look like the next year and the next as the green leaked away?

Over a ten-year span, starting in 1998, mountain pine beetles gradually infested over 3 million acres in western Montana, killing over 31 million host trees. University of Montana forestry professor Diana Six defined this beetle outbreak as "unprecedented in size and severity." Such attacks are cyclical, with the last major attack noted in the 1970s and 80s of my childhood. That outbreak peaked in 1982 at just over two million infested acres and lasted another ten years.

I brought my husband and his children to my family cabin in 1999, their first time in Montana, just as the next beetle outbreak cycle began. I took vicarious pleasure as they all enjoyed the view of the limestone cliffs, the dense forest, the clear Smith River teeming with browns and rainbows and, for the luckiest of anglers, an occasional cutthroat or brookie. We fished, we hiked, we tubed the river, we stayed up late watching for shooting stars and the shimmering green curtain of aurora borealis.

The cabin is a small, primitive dwelling hewn of pines from the mountainside, originally sealed with black tar that eventually thinned and cracked, leaving small holes, open invitations for insects of every kind. Once, lying on the bed for an afternoon nap, I noticed points of light piercing from between logs like tiny stars, and I knew it was past time for repairs. We patched the tar and finally coated everything with putty that hardened to look like peanut butter spread by a child. Sloppy, but effective.

The cabin wasn't built to impress and can't compete with half-million- dollar summer homes in the picturesque, gated canyon. But it's historic, the first in the canyon, built by a hunter who left behind a box of steel leg traps, a moth-eaten, dusty black bear skin, and bobcat pelts that I don't remember because they were stolen when I was a kid. My husband wanted the cabin and the lifestyle he imagined came with it. After my grandfather's death, my family didn't use the cabin, but they didn't sell, knowing they'd see me and their future grandchildren more often if my fisherman had access to the Smith River. We drove 1800 miles from our home in Pennsylvania every summer. We stayed four or five weeks then drove 1800 miles back. We drove first with his teenagers and then our infants, six of us with luggage and fly rods in an SUV.

In 2009 he convinced me to broker a deal with my mother and her siblings. I hesitated as I imagined all the places I would never visit, our vacation money sunk into cabin taxes and repairs. I balked when he suggested the first asking price was too high and that I needed to convince my family to knock it down by a third. But I did it, and soon his name was beside mine on the deed.

Years later, reading through old journals, I discovered something I'd written while on vacation at the cabin: "[he's] still angling for us to buy this place...and I waver on that, loving the scenery and the memories but not seeing anything practical in trying to maintain property from two thousand miles away." I wrote that five years before the sales contract was signed, before I convinced myself I could trade this property for a level of emotional security that seemed always out of reach.

Parasitism is a relationship that benefits one creature at the expense of another. It is not symbiotic and cannot, by definition, be mutual. Still, most parasites thrive as long as their hosts do. In the case of the mountain pine beetle, the species thrives by slowly choking the life from its host.

When literary scholars defined deconstructionists as "parasites" on literature, J. Hillis Miller's response in "The Critic as Host" focused on the word's etymology meaning "beside" and "food," demonstrating how parasite originally meant someone who shares food alongside another. Host, likewise, has multiple meanings: stranger and guest, stranger and enemy. Host and hostile share a root meaning: shared space and sustenance can be relationship or invasion.

The vast acreage of red, brown, and gray trees, their hue determined by their stage of dying, are called "kill zones" or, depending on whether one privileges the point of view of the parasite or the host, "dead zones." The beetles bore through the outer bark of their favorite hosts -- lodgepole pine and ponderosa pine -- in autumn, and each of the females lays about 75 eggs. Then the budding beetles go through several stages, building up glycol, a kind of antifreeze compound, as the temperatures drop. Once that process is complete, mountain pine beetle larvae can tolerate long periods of extreme cold.

Climate change has been a key contributing factor in these zones of destruction. I have sometimes said I hate winter. I have imagined retiring where snow exists only on Christmas cards. I have failed to appreciate how crucial dramatic cold snaps are to ecological balance. Winter freeze kills some things to save others. Morphing mountain pine beetles will only die if winter starts early enough with temperatures falling below zero. My joy over a mild winter, of the many mild winters that herald global warming, becomes the loss of millions of acres of forest.

Mountain pine beetles start at the bottom of their favorite host trees, boring into the bark and into the resin, creating pitch tubes, a mix of resin and boring dust where eggs can be laid. The healthiest trees in non-drought years can effectively flush out the beetles with strong pitch flow, resulting in an unsuccessful infestation. In drought years, which are most years in the American West, when there simply isn't enough pitch in the tree, those telltale tubes aren't there, and an invasion can only be identified by very fine sawdust in the crevices of the bark. It takes an expert eye to notice these "blind attacks."

Once an invasion of beetles reaches the core of the tree, give it up for lost. When the flow of nutrients is cut off, the core shrivels, leaving a dry and vulnerable tree ready to topple. The risk of dramatic, widespread summer wildfires increases in high "dead zone" areas. Firefighters cannot be on the ground where blazing trees send temperatures soaring as they rapidly burn and fall. The safest response is to give up more acres: controlled burns that sacrifice vast stretches of individual trees to save the whole forest. More fire means more carbon in the atmosphere. Warmer climate. More beetles surviving and invading more trees.

This spiraling cycle of destruction.

The trees are not willing hosts. They do not lay out the welcome mat for parasites or open tiny doors in their trunks. The beetles simply like what a certain type of tree offers. My ex-husband has his own type. His girlfriend reminds me of the me who first met him: a Taurus who drives a Prius, has advanced degrees but no children, and is unbelievably accommodating to whatever he wants.

I was a willing host. I never expected my invited guest to try to possess me and mine. But then I also believed our relationship was mutual, symbiotic. And I failed to recognize my own vulnerability to invasion. I met my husband before I'd fully untangled from my first love, a young man who desperately wanted our relationship one day and desperately wanted out the next. After all that anguish and heartbreak, I was primed for something solid and stable. I needed to invent secure companionship where there was only slow invasion.

In a journal from my first year dating my husband, I noted with irritation that he wanted a detailed schedule of my planned time at a four-day conference across the country. I wrote, "He says he just wants to share my experience. It feels more invasive than that." And then I stayed another thirteen years. I didn't pay attention to the slow choking of my own pitch flow until the core was threatened. But some part of me refused to dry up and die and, unlike an infested tree, I could, with great difficulty, uproot myself.

Parasites are opportunistic. Show vulnerability and a glimpse of the resources they want or need, and they'll take them. Open the door to your cabin, your life, and they will presume ownership.

Emily Post, that maven of good manners, advises that a good host is hospitable, warm, and gracious. Why the celebration of the "gracious host" who smiles as parasitic guests consume everything on the table?

In the case of Christ, the body is on the table. The Host. In Catholic tradition, when we consume the Host, we devour the actual flesh of our god.

Post reminds us that a host must make her guests feel comfortable and welcome. The Church reminds us that we must aspire to be Christ-like. I tried to conduct myself like a good host when my ex-husband brought his new girlfriend to our cabin while I was there on vacation. The summer before, when we'd split, we'd also split time at the cabin, trading the children in Montana where my parents still lived. Early that next summer, when I'd taken a new administrative position, I told him I didn't know if I'd make it to Montana or not, and we left it at that.

After I'd negotiated terms with my employer, I sent an e-mail with the dates I'd be there on my vacation with the boys and suggestions for how and where to trade them for his vacation. He responded that my plan wouldn't work, that he'd already invited friends to the cabin that first week. Our next exchanges went something like this:

Me: Then uninvite them. This is the only time I can come.

Him: I can't. They've bought plane tickets. It would be rude.

Me: Then I'm happy to meet your friends since I'll be there at that time. It's my cabin too.

Him: They don't want to meet you.

Me: I'm sorry to hear you have the kind of friends who want to drive me out of my own cabin and be so rude as to not meet me.

What is rude? What is polite? What are the benefits to either? I finally caught on that these were not "friends," but a singular friend, a new girlfriend about whom he'd told me nothing. When he finally confessed what I suspected, likely hoping I would give up, I held my ground. When he said he wasn't ready for the boys to meet this woman, expecting me to solve that problem, I held my ground.

I was not, after all, a tree, and I had given up enough. I'd surrendered to him my home and all its accumulated furnishings. I'd compromised on custody issues, sometimes against my better judgment. I'd given up money, valued friendships, and all but a few scraps of dignity. Exchanges I hoped would purchase peace between us, but always he wanted the next thing. And the next.

I did not begrudge him his own vacation time with the boys at the cabin, but I would not give up my claim to mine. My friends and family thought he was bluffing, but I knew better by then.

I left my young sons with their grandparents. I drove to the cabin where I settled in and waited for hours, my music playing, my computer open as I tried, and failed, to fill the tense hours with writing. Around five o'clock I heard, then saw, the black SUV at the gate. My heart thrashed in my chest.

Once something invades your space, it's difficult to root out, especially if it multiplies exponentially. When a sealed bag of walnuts concealing the eggs of the Mediterranean flour moth made its way into a cupboard, my kitchen was soon overrun with tiny, dun-colored moths fluttering out of dark crevices. I killed the larvae, trying to eliminate them before they ate their way in or out of plastic bags of nuts and grains. I dumped every bag of flour and cereal with the telltale webbing, and I cleaned with bleach and set out pheromone traps. And still a moth would flutter by in the corner of my vision.

When my ex-husband and his new girlfriend entered the main room of the cabin, I said to her, "You're welcome here. I hope you enjoy your visit." Then, "It's him I'm pissed at."

How to be a good host? How to love and demonstrate openness in the face of such careless-ness? Christian philosophy asks that we turn the other cheek. Common wisdom says that if you give someone an inch, he'll think he's a ruler. Mythology advises that some bloodsuckers can only enter your home if invited. The crucial difference between the lodgepole pine's parasite and mine is that I welcomed my visitor, unaware of how much of my life would be slowly strangled. The beetle simply bores in, incapable of human greed or malice. The larvae feast on their host all winter long then, when spring temperatures rise, the mature beetles eat their way back out of the used and dying tree and migrate in search of new resources.

They brought in their groceries, cramming their milk next to mine in the dorm size fridge, setting a bag of cherries atop my bag of cherries. He opened a cabinet and held up a bag of flour from the summer before. He asked if it was still good. I said, "Sure." She wrinkled her nose and said, "I wouldn't use that," and so he tossed it in the trash.

They decided to go fishing before dark. I remained at the old oak table where my grandparents had played hundreds of games of pinochle. My computer was still open, and I just wrote a few words and waited, wrote a few more and waited, trying to avoid looking at the two double beds a couple feet apart, wondering if they really would stay, if I would. The sun slipped past the canyon walls.

When they returned, they stood over the table where I was rooted, my laptop open between us like a shield. "We need to know when you're leaving," they said. "This is uncomfortable."

I laughed aloud, the nervous laugh of a host detecting the first signs of social disaster. I mustered courage and told her that this was between him and me, that she could wait outside. She did. That left me where I really didn't want to be: alone with a bully who was only a bully when we were alone. He loomed over me, face red with embarrassment, then fury. I remember no details of the verbal blast that followed, just that the focus was on my own wretched and mean-spirited nature. I'd heard it before, and I held my ground until I couldn't. I fled to the front porch, shaking and weeping while they consulted in private then went back inside to pack.

Gathering their groceries, he asked, "Which cherries are ours?" She replied, "The good ones."

I spent the night alone, sleepless and weeping until my stomach cramped, this victory feeling anything but. In the morning, I left a note on the kitchen table advising them that I was in town until the next day, that I'd return with the boys, and that they were not welcome to be there during my vacation time. And when I returned, the note was gone. So were they. When guests are no longer guests, but parasites, a scourge on your well-being and a threat to your very life, you must show them the door, insist they exit, then lock the door. Forever.

That part is harder than I wish it were. Legally, the cabin that had been in my family for over forty years now belongs to us both. And I willingly agreed to that, dickered down the price, stealing from my own family to satisfy a greed not my own. But I am not the cabin, and the cabin is not me. I am not him, and he is not me. In a parasitic relationship, those boundaries must be very clear. If not, you lose yourself, dried to tinder waiting for a lightning strike.

Climate change has taken a toll on the forests of Montana and much of the West. The thinning of the forest of weaker, older trees is actually beneficial to forests. But the beetles, thriving in warmer than usual winters, eventually migrate to attack healthy trees.

Because of greenhouse gases like carbon dioxide and methane, the average temperature on the planet is expected to rise between 1.8 and 4.0 degrees Celsius throughout the twenty-first century. With warmer winters, insect populations increase, snow packs decrease. Less snow means less water, which stresses trees, making them more susceptible to infestations. And so scientists are predicting more dramatic changes in western coniferous forests, including the killing of trees at higher-than-usual elevations and a shift in which species of trees are targeted, as choice hosts become scarcer. When some types of pines are killed, they are replaced by other trees and plants that attract different animals and insects, the entire ecological landscape changing.

Here's what I can't resolve: my need to judge those changes, to understand them as "good" or "bad" exists in order to alleviate the anxiety that change itself creates. The planet has been evolving since long before humans inhabited it. The Smith River canyon undergoes human development every summer: new million dollar cabins with more space and amenities than the home I live in year-round, one wealthy owner rerouting the only road leading from mountain to meadow to accommodate a new horse corral and keep road dust away from his deck. Motorbikes and ATVs, once forbidden by owner agreement, now rip through the meadow and the quiet. Mountain lions: tracked and shot. The beaver dam torn down by anglers, rebuilt elsewhere, demolished by flooding. A helicopter pad constructed a couple miles around the river bend so the man known as "the Californian" can fly in and out at will.

I can easily become self-righteous about parasites until I wonder how mutual this human and earth relationship really is as we purchase, fence, steal, mine, and undermine the very place that gives us life. I, too, am a parasite exploiting my benevolent host.

The cabin itself changes year after year: the roof went from reflective, blinding tin when I was a kid to dull shingles that curled up and cracked, to a new, plum-colored tin after hail destroyed the previous roof. A front porch was added and has been painted and repainted a few times. Fireplace rebuilt, shed attached to the backside, new outhouse dug, old one filled in and capped. We had horses when I was a kid, a statuesque white horse named Shadow and a plump, fussy mare we called Dolly. Then the winters became too severe, and the Californian didn't want horses foraging on his property, and they were sold.

Now a strange pair of women's boots, too large for me, waits smugly inside the storm door. The detritus of my grandparents' summers here--ball caps, cowboy statues, vintage tins--remain piled by the door like trash. Once, before we split up, I saw that my husband had taken my grandfather's small soap dish printed with a buxom woman and a sexist saying and hung it in his office like a prop. When I saw it 1800 miles from where I believed it belonged, I was angry, as if in that moment, I had tangible proof of pieces of my history being stolen away. Unimportant pieces, if I'm being honest. But we hadn't even bought the cabin yet, and now I think of this moment as a test, the first small claim staked. And, like many things, I just let it go to preserve the peace, sacrificing the trees for the forest.

Some things I can't give up, even when it seems the struggle isn't worth it. One year, infuriated about my claim on cabin time, he made me meet him in Rapid City, South Dakota to exchange the children, even though he knew I was at my parents', forty miles from the cabin. By the time I picked up the boys in a Denny's parking lot, they'd spent five weeks in Montana. They didn't want to travel nine hours back or even see the cabin again, and I scrambled for new plans to salvage our time together. We went to relatives in Denver, but after children's museums and trampoline parks and Chuck E. Cheese, I needed quiet, living nature. I drove us to Rocky Mountain National Park, nestled in a region where more than 1.5 million acres of forest have been destroyed by the mountain pine beetle. Halfway through Trail Ridge Road, we stopped at a gift shop, pricey and cluttered with beautiful, hand-crafted objects meant as souvenir slivers of the grand wonder of the park, which you can't take home except in flat photos and shifting memory. I have always been drawn to objects, infusing them with meaning to the detriment of my crowded house.

There, in August, snow clinging to the rocks around the shop's parking area, I saw a hand-turned bowl made from a beetle-killed tree. The coloring streaked through the wood grain, the sign explained, came from the blue-stain fungus the beetles leave in the tree, and the wood-worker saw the opportunity to create something beautiful from something destroyed. I bought it.

By the time I returned to the Smith River Canyon, the view from the top of the canyon road had changed, everything wider and more open. As I slowly wound a rented SUV down and around the switchbacks, I noted the cut and blackened logs stacked roadside. Gaps opened where pine had once towered, dotted now with the limp-leaved weed known as mullein, stalks too feeble to hold the eroding soil from its inevitable slide down the slope.

At the cabin, I parked the Jeep in the shade of the pines and stepped into the dry meadow grass, inhaling clean mountain air, scanning the limestone cliffs and healthy pine. The neighbor wandered up from his cabin for his seasonal check-in and update, and I asked why I didn't see any beetle-killed trees.

"Cut those down," he said, explaining that lightning had started a small fire atop the mountain, the dead trees the tinder. A volunteer fire department in White Sulphur Springs, forty-five miles away by gravel road, had prevented the fire from spreading, and the cabin association had removed the rest of the dead and dying trees along our side of the river. "Sure changes the view," he noted. He meant the log stacks I'd seen on the side of the mountain road.

"I mean over there," I said, pointing across the river to the Lewis & Clark National Forest. "It's all green."

"You're just not seeing the dead ones," he noted before waving and heading back to his cabin, never one for a lot of talk. I stared over to the mountainside, lush with pine that, at a distance, looked like a painting of trees--blurry, soft, variously sunlit and shadowed. I looked again and saw, there, a skeleton of a tree, gray and bare of needles. Then another, and, as my eyes adjusted, I could squint and make out a couple more, hidden in an otherwise healthy, recovered forest.

In the few years I was away from the canyon, the red and brown needles had all dropped off, the damage invisible unless you wanted to see it. There were still a few reddish trees left. One rusty sentinel stood stubborn, high on a cliff across the river from the front of the cabin, greeting me every time I opened the door. I tried to take a photo of it, evidence of the changes that had once seemed so threatening, but all anyone else notices is the wide view--blue sky, white clouds, towering green pines, and the ever-eroding limestone cliffs full of fossil imprints of the sea that used to be.

ROLE REVERSAL

by Catherine Wald

Disappointed?

Hell, yeah.
Deal was,
she was supposed
to go before he did – fade
languidly like a 19th
Century tubercular in
a frilly nightdress --
precious coddled
princess to the end.

Watching the help tend
to him on his deathbed,
she tries to conceal
her rage beneath
something that looks
like grief.

She will never
forgive
him.

TRUE LOVE NEVER DIES

by Beth Jordan

True love never dies. Never. It grows stronger as each day passes. Dreams are shared, promises made. *Whatever happens in the future, I shall always have you.*

Cherished vows shared on a special day long ago--that day, the day all my dreams came true, still reigns as the happiest in my life.

My heart is no longer my own. The fickle organ beats now just to hear the sound of his voice and his alone. His touch comforts me and soothes away the troubles of the day. Our shared dreams for the future are intertwined all the way down to the rocking chairs on the front porch when old age comes knocking.

I still remember the warm sense of belonging when he came up behind me, curled his arms around my waist and whispered, "I got you," into my ear. My whole world existed in his eyes. When he walked into the room or answered the phone, I smiled at the miracle that brought him into my life. A wonder incarnate whose arms I woke up in every morning and rushed home to each evening. He added meaning and substance where there had only been existence before.

If I glanced up at any given time and caught him watching me, I experienced a sudden sharp feeling in the region of my heart. It was exultant, but the swiftness and depth of it resembled pain. I am pierced straight through by cupid's arrow and flinch at the rapturous sensation. My breath caught, my heart raced, and my lips hungered for the taste of him. My intensity came from knowing in my heart he felt exactly the same.

Our friends ask us how we do it. Couples around us drift apart, move on, and ask for our secret. The secret is compromise, I tell them. Love bound us together, forever changing "me" into "we."I no longer have to face the world alone, with its constant stumbling blocks. Together, we could face anything this old world dished out.

Maybe going to a basketball game with my husband isn't my first choice of what to do on a Saturday night, but attending that fundraiser with me last month wasn't his either.

Once, I snagged tickets to Phantom of the Opera from a friend at work who couldn't attend. My favorite--it's so romantic.I knew he would rather stuff his fist into an operating garbage disposal than attend. I promised to get up at dawn on Saturday morning and go fishing with him and followed up with temptations like cold beer in the cooler, baiting my own hook, and cleaning my catch myself. He held my hand against his chest during the opera. That's love. That's compromise. That's commitment.

Then, later in our marriage, came the moment when I realized I hadn't caught him watching me in a long while. He hadn't inquired about my day for weeks, and just that morning he wondered aloud if I planned to go out dressed like that. Lurking in the shadows of happiness could be an unwanted visitor. This interloper showed up striking like a bolt of lightning, causing as much damage. Had I basked in love's glory recklessly assuming the gift mine to keep? Another kind of arrow had struck my love squarely in the heart. This arrow's poison seemed to be killing his love for me.

I called my mom daily pleading for advice. My parents had weathered a marital storm or two in their day. She will know what to do.

"Give him time and space and he'll come around. Sometimes men are under a lot of pressure."

Her words soothed me for a time. I took on more of the household duties to relieve my loved one.

Cleaning one day, I found a lease contract on his desk for an apartment located four blocks from our house. Cupid's arrow morphed into a white- hot, smoldering spike through my soul.

A tidal wave of pain washed over me while inwardly I curled into the fetal position. Something beautiful beyond imagination now showed signs of gangrene. Why didn't I notice it sooner? What did I do wrong? How can I save this marriage? I have enough love for the both of us. Is there someone else? Questions and my imagination torture me as I contort myself trying to please him and win his affection back. My fear of his answers keeps my questions locked inside. The answers might be way beyond what a movie and popcorn can repair.

Then he stopped coming home for dinner; he had to work late. After all, he just started his own business.

Where has he gone, my lover, companion, confessor and helpmate? Wherever he went, my best friend resides there too. How can I face the future without my trusty sidekick?

Now when I called, my mom cried with me. She begged me to confront him, preserve my dignity and face the inevitable.

"It's best to face life's problems head on and rise above it." In the next breath, she added, "He never deserved you."

That's what moms are supposed to say, I thought. She doesn't understand. Love needs tender gardening, lots of sunshine and plenty of water. The yield could be abundant.

Weeks drag by. I suggested a vacation, bought new lingerie and cooked all his favorites. I try one desperate move after another to reclaim what we had, but it's a changed landscape, unfamiliar territory, and he is not sharing any details with me.

On our sixteenth wedding anniversary, he invited me out to dinner at my favorite restaurant. It boasted a five-star rating with a three-month waiting list. I had looked forward to it for weeks. I read all kinds of happy thoughts into the gesture. Maybe he's decided this team is the best there is after all. I bought a new dress and sexy shoes for the occasion. I did my hair the way he loved it best and bought him a Rolex watch. I wrapped it in blue gift paper--his favorite color. It was our anniversary after all.

After the waiter had set the mouth-watering entrees in front of us, my lover said he had something important to tell me.

He wanted a divorce.

The realization washed over me that we were at my favorite restaurant to avoid a scene. It was over. I sat stunned into silence while he babbled on about the legalities of our marital death. I had spent the first four years of our marriage working to put him through law school.

I interrupted him, "Why are you doing this?" Unable to control them, tears ran down my face.

He pulled a folded sheath of papers from his breast pocket and slid them toward me on the table. Shrugging his shoulders, he said, "I'm done."He pushed his meal aside and sat back in his chair. His body language more than his words conveyed his message.

I'm done. Spoken with venom. Like those two words explained everything. My mind flashed to our wedding day when he took my hand and told me he'd never let go. *How did I offend you? Forgive me, please?* My eyes searched his face in vain for signs of the man I loved. *Where have you gone?*

"If you change your mind and want to come home, please do, because I will always love you." I hoped my declaration reached my lover's ears buried somewhere deep inside the stranger before me.

His smile wilted before reaching his eyes. "Don't count on it."

After his departure, I sat there stunned thinking about the first time I met him, the moment I fell in love, our wedding day, and wondered how I would function this day forward with only half a heart. The other half belonged to him. It would always belong to him. How do you turn off a heart? How do you tell it to stop loving? How do you cut out the traitorous, cancerous beast from your chest? It's not recyclable.

I cried in the car driving home and cried for years afterward. I never heard a word from him again. I couldn't sleep without him to snuggle up to and began taking prescription sleeping meds. My nightly dreams were twisted versions of me pleading with him, and him laughing in my face, assuming I got any sleep at all.

Mom begged me to come home to recover in the loving arms of family. But my heart belonged here.

His father had died five years before our divorce and left a fortune to my husband. Perhaps he thought he no longer needed the woman who had put him through law school, helped him start his business and loved him more than anyone else in the world.

I heard he found a twenty-something girlfriend who was on his payroll, but no one had ever met her. Still, my love didn't die. I could tell by the constant pain that wracked me.

Since everything we owned resided in a trust containing my husband's fortune, my lawyer and the judge informed me I was entitled to absolutely nothing. The house, cars, furniture, even the dog, were legally his. I was allowed to pack my clothes and leave. After sixteen years of marriage, I left the love of my life behind and waited for my next paycheck to make a security deposit on an apartment. Confident he would call to offer help, I kept my cell phone tucked under my bra strap, but he never called.

My parents sent money to help me get back on my feet. Their checks arrived with notes filled with love and encouragement. And the same postscript every time--please come home.

As the years passed, my former witty, happy and energetic personality slipped further and further away. Loved ones and friends alike offered adages meant to encourage, but hollow people can't hear. The desperate pray for a miracle, as I did daily. My abused heart, like any other victim, cried out for its life force but was denied.

I couldn't hang out with our friends because they were "our" friends. I lost touch with them and shut myself off from the world. They wouldn't miss me. No one would miss me, I told myself.

Sixteen years had passed since the finalization of my divorce. My mother's cancer came out of remission, and she required hospice care. For the last twelve months of her life, I served as her hospice nurse the third week of every month. My siblings took turns in my absence. I couldn't make up my mind. Should I pray for a miracle? Or pray she goes quickly and in peace? Were my prayers for her or me? I dreamt of folding myself into his arms and finding the comfort denied me.

My beloved had promised we would get through everything together. After standing beside him and helping him through the tragedy of his parents' deaths, he was nowhere to be found when my mom lost her twenty-year battle with melanoma. I lost my mother four years ago. As I stood over her grave, I cursed my lost love for his absence instead of sending her off with the loving prayer she deserved. And in the next breath prayed God would send him back to me.

A deep depression claimed me after my mother's death. I saw a psychiatrist in the hope he had a silver bullet for the traitorous half of my heart. Maybe then I could move on with my life. He prescribed anti- depressants and suggested counseling.

I learned that counselors don't know how to kill love either. They suggested options to try. Take walks. Write in a journal. Make some new friends. Keep busy. Learn something new. Find your passion in life.

I took walks, but while walking, I thought about him. How many times did I ask my journal why he left? Budding friendships didn't want to hear about my emotional baggage, and somehow I couldn't keep it out of conversations. I worked, spent quality time with my daughter who had been abandoned by him as well, and watched over my incomparable grandchildren. I learned how to can vegetables and fruits and to make homemade jellies and jams. And I learned that my great passion in life was the husband I had lost.

Without my mom, my pain found no outlet. It threatened to engulf me. In his absence, I had grown even closer to my mother sharing with her all I would have shared with him.

Everyone says time will heal the wounds, but no one knows how much time. Five years? Ten years? Twenty years? There are wounds that never heal. I had tried to explain that to all my previous counselors. How does betrayal heal? Isn't it always a betrayal? Time doesn't change that. Betrayal doesn't wake up one day and cast off its shroud to be replaced by devotion. Betrayal festers like an infected wound. You can smell it rotting over the years. There's no hiding it.

I did learn one thing from my counselor--hate is the other side of love. And because hate has an inverse relation to love, it only proved my point. I loved him still.

Parents are the only people in the world who love you no matter what. There is nothing you could do that would cause them to stop loving you. I thought about that, and I owed my beloved mother a letter. In it, I told her how much I had missed her and our daily talks.

There was a long list of things I missed; her advice, not getting her recipes right, her laughter, her hugs, our shopping trips, our lunches out, our vacations together, people mistaking us for sisters, and the family referring to me as Kathleen's oldest. She was my tear-jerker movie buddy. I remembered how she would tell me repeatedly that that man wasn't good enough for me. Always the personal cheerleader. (You were right, Mom.) What did she see that I couldn't?

Before she died, she would drop whatever she had been doing to talk to me. I wrote sheet after sheet until my legal pad ran out of paper. Every scrap piece of paper I could find in the house served my purpose on its reverse side.

Suddenly, the power of journaling hit me full force, and a burning cloak of shame engulfed me. Tears ran down my face, and a sharp pain throbbed at my temple. But I had succeeded in committing the whole story to paper, the death of a marriage and a testament to enduring love, and it had come to an epiphany. On those pages, right there in front of me, existed the proof I needed to save myself. The beginning of the missive contained a few pages where I lamented over my long-lost marriage, and then the massive tome that followed revealed a thousand ways I loved and missed my mother. The myriad ways she had shown her love to me had never wavered a single day. The death of my marriage did not mean the death of my soul. My soul still lived and loved as I never thought it would again. Hours passed--it seemed like hours--as I sat there, my head in my hands, sobbing my heart out. What a fool I had been. I had short-changed my mother's unwavering love and devotion because of him, the unworthy. Twenty desolate years had passed while I tormented myself over his absence obsessing over why--why did he leave me? I finally concluded why he left didn't matter. The cold, hard fact was he no longer loved me.

Maybe he experienced a mid-life crisis, needed a bigger house, and a trophy wife to go with his legal practice. Maybe I didn't fit into the new social circles he pictured for himself. Whatever the reason, he had evolved into someone I no longer recognized. And if I'm honest with myself, I didn't love the man he'd become. I was in love with the man I married; a man who no longer existed.

And just like that, after twenty long years, the chains that had bound me to him fell away, and the burden lifted from my shoulders. In the time it takes to snap your fingers, I reclaimed my heart. The delusion evaporated.

I remembered all the helpful hints, coaching and downright prodding my mother employed over the years in the effort to jolt me out of my misery. I didn't listen. I never listened. I waited. I was always waiting for him. He would come back. Love this strong can't be wrong. I was right, but about the wrong person.

The answer I had been looking for all this time was indeed love. Allowing myself to experience the purity and depth of a lifetime of my mother's love revealed to me what true love is, what it should feel like, act like, and look like. Love is a powerful force that teaches us a lot about ourselves and others. In the end, the power of my mother's love saved me.

On a beautiful spring day, I drove 385 miles to my mother's grave in a military graveyard in southern Maryland and laid the letter on her tombstone weighing it down with a rock. My fingers traced the letters of her name carved into the stone. Underneath, it said beloved wife and mother. I smiled at the understatement.

"Hello, Mom. I'm home. I love and miss you. Today I have a prayer for you straight from my heart."

She lives on in my heart. Death can't take that away. I knew I didn't have to ask for her forgiveness.

MY BIOME

by Rehana Campbell

Swirling dust particles shimmer as they dance,
Flashing their smiles like an early summer dawn.
I reach my hand out to play with the minerals,
But as I come near they all dart aside.

I am surrounded by it, I am confounded by it,
I am flattened by the knowing,
Showing twenty-seven years of blue iris blossom from my windows.
Doesn't it look breathtakingly beautiful?
I cleaned up just for you,
You should not see the filth, the black garbage bags.
They rot in my basement unless I get rid of them,
They stick to my baseboards and grow roots, as well.

Nowadays, those streams don't rapidly run elsewhere.

Instead they glimmer softly, paddling on,
Drifting inwards, swiftly falling.
Life gravitating toward life,
That is what the air echoed,
That is what the soil planted.
That is what the trees breathed.

THE OTHER SIDE

by Debbie Weingarten

The afternoon brings long rays of sun through the window, and specks of dust float around us like stars. We live in a home the size of a postage stamp, and it is full of a baby and a toddler, a broken mama, one dog, one cat-- all growing, healing, mucking through the days together.

I have begun to think in motivational phrases:

Orient towards the light. Take a step. Repeat.

If you're going through hell, keep going.

We are never given anything more than we can handle.

This is a brand new year, I say to myself, through the lull of the afternoon. The baby stretches in his sleep, as if he knows that new years are for waking up.

With the second child, time does not seem quite so cavernous. It's like walking a familiar path, recognizing this crooked tree, or that patch of wildflowers, or the wooden bridge just beyond the rhododendron. The baby will cut teeth, learn to walk, say "bird" and "dog," sprout little blonde hairs on his legs, ride a tricycle, finally sleep through the night. And I-- tired rings below my eyes, yoga pants for days-- will marvel at how time has somehow robbed us and kept us prisoner at the very same time.

I could feel the divorce before it came. It circled us for two long years, disguised as stress from sleep deprivation, an infant, a demanding business. It has been a year since I woke up to the abuse and control, since my son and I fled in our pajamas, the baby still the size of a fist in my belly.

I have been ushering us through the weeks, each one its own journey and wall of grief, each one bringing new layers of deconstruction, clarity, documents from the lawyer. For a time, I am set adrift on my own solitary raft, letting the warm ocean wash over me. I am tired of crying, and I cannot eat. Instead, I spend time sorting through all of the lies told to me so casually. I turn them over like seashells, put them in a bucket, scream. It is all one big mindfuck.

I have embraced things I was never allowed: a frivolous coffee routine, afternoon naps, frozen foods, shitty milkshakes. I find comfort from things I never thought I would: signs of synchronicity, self-help books, kind sister strangers, internet support groups, old songs with new meanings.

Today we are on the other side-- the side of golden afternoons and dust specks. Sometimes I want to cry simply because I am so proud to have made it through. The kids play together on the floor. They dump out Legos with such joy, line up toy cars, empty the folded laundry from the basket so the toddler can make a fort. Toys and clothes are flying everywhere, and I am letting it all happen, because how do you stop a hurricane? The toddler growls like a lion and sends the basket careening across the floor. The baby squeals.

My memories fold into one another. They present as an accordion of images, sensory details colliding and sometimes remaining just beyond my grasp-- I am like a child on a stool reaching for the light switch. But certain things I remember so vividly that they seem to catch in some miswired part of my brain, like a track on repeat:

> the smell of onions sautéing in coconut oil, the stink of a cast iron left to soak too long, the souring of goat milk, the blue of a bedroom, the white bellies of dogs, dried pigweed in my boots, the blur of headlights on the highway, winter seeping in through cracks in the wall, the smell of dead chickens, Regina Spektor singing *your hair was long when we first met*, my ex-husband holding me down and saying *you're crazy, you're a bitch, you're a stupid white cunt.*

The baby wants to be held, so I put him on my back in the Ergo. The weight of a baby has become so familiar. We dance together in the kitchen, gathering red lentils, celery, garlic, one lonely onion. We chop. We sway. I set a pan on the stove and then step on a plastic dinosaur with one bare foot. I am brought to laughing, cursing tears. The Pandora station plays John Prine, and his voice finds a wound inside my chest. For a moment, I want to crawl back under the covers, but I let the music crack me open instead.

> *Blow up your TV, throw away your paper,*
> *Go to the country, build you a home,*
> *Plant a little garden, eat a lot of peaches,*
> *Try and find Jesus on your own.*

It does not hurt like touching a stove or skinning a knee. It hurts in a raw chest kind of way. Like sitting at the top of Gates Pass and staring down at the saguaros, all lined up like thousands of soldiers. It hurts like finding a baby bird dried up on the sidewalk. It hurts like how beautiful it is to watch my toddler belly-laugh. It hurts like knowing someone is dying safe and in their sleep.

A year is a long string of tiny moments:

> One day we are leaving in our pajamas, getting the fuck out, drawing a line.
>
> Five months later, I am rooted to the bathroom floor. The faces coo. Hands smooth my hair in the yellow light. I am a white belly, round as a planet, a screaming head. When finally, the baby slips out from between my legs, so too slips the pain, the sadness, all of the fear.
>
> A year later, we are swaying to John Prine in a doll-sized kitchen. The toddler is melting down because a piece of rice is stuck in his hair, and the baby is crying and pulling on my shirt, and my milk is letting down all over the place. We are so overdue for sleep that everyone is irrational and my chin keeps dropping to my chest.

We pile into the rocking chair. The toddler reaches out to hold his brother's hand. *We sing You Are My Sunshine*, except we say "when skies are blue" instead of "gray," because that's the way we like it best. I think, *maybe I'm doing this whole single mom thing okay*.

Each night when I fall asleep, I envision the home we will have someday. Worn wooden floors for my wood-starved bare feet, built-in cabinets, morning light. A kitchen with enough space for a table and chairs, a long counter for chopping and all necessary coffee supplies. Tinctures, oils, spices spilling out of their hiding places. Crayon art on the walls. Orchids and wooden trains tucked in the windowsill. Cactus bones and bicycles in the yard. And two beautiful sons who grow up knowing that a mother is fireproof, a strongbox, a shelter. That a woman is a wild wonderful thing--never to be owned, kept, or silenced.

Originally published in the Manifest-Station

A GLITTERING OF HUMMINGBIRDS, A CHARM

by Chauna Craig

"I am the knife and the wound it deals."
–Charles Baudelaire

Walk to the beach everyday. This self-prescription, a pledge I can keep. The northern, rocky beach of Orcas Island is a quarter mile from the artists' residency, with clear day views of Lummi Island and Mount Baker. On fog-drenched mornings I can still see and hear the slate waves lapping, mergansers adrift, bobbing unbothered by winter waters. I sort rocks in the rain, pick over driftwood and snail shells, their rigid lips plugged with pebbles impossible to spit out. I listen to the hypnotic buzzing of light aircraft ascending over the sea. Focus on these, and my mind settles awhile.

This is not a nature essay. Except that every essay is an inquiry into the nature of something.

A hummingbird emerges from the bluing dawn outside the window, bowing its head to the feeder. This may be the tiniest bird I've ever seen. Cup it in my hands and its wings could still flutter. One moment the bird appears dull, monochromatic as rain, but the next slight turn, a fiery jewel. I begin to doubt what I see, but the bird book tells me I've just met Anna's hummingbird, a species that doesn't leave the island.

The night before I left Pittsburgh for the Olympic Peninsula, fear spread its first tendrils around my heart, which convulsed, trying to shake off the sickness, the building dread. I thought about canceling. I told myself to stop. *Please* stop. Not this again.

Six years earlier, I'd left someone whose all-consuming self left no space for empathy, even when I was at my most needy. I no longer recognized myself--anxious and depressed and so dull. I'd been awarded a month-long residency in Vermont where I intended to write, return to myself and then to an apartment I'd leased in secret. Only I felt disloyal and guilty and told him anyway, calling it my "summer writing studio," a farce we both pretended to believe until I slipped and mentioned the two bedrooms.

There are children on the edges of this story. And they make it impossible to tell this story. They also make it impossible not to.

He told his first set of children, whom I'd helped raise, that their mother had abandoned them. I imagined the trio as victims in a fairy tale--

a lonely woodcutter and his two children starving for love in a cottage deep in the forest. Who could counter this sad story when he had custody and she lived in another state? Who wouldn't pity this man the burden of single parenthood and its companion, loneliness? Then, I still believed I could trust the evidence someone else laid out for me.

On my third morning at the beach, I perch on a boulder to meditate on the waves and notice what appear to be the legs of a crab rising from the water. Squinting, I recognize the feet of a sea bird cramped and curled like claws. Slapping waves from a boat's wake raise one drab, bedraggled wing like a greeting. Not waving, but drowning. Not drowning, but drowned.

The hummingbird chooses the only feeder that appears empty. Sugar junkie craving the syrupy sludge at the bottom. Head raised after a long drink, its body forms a vector from sleek tail to needle bill, poised like an arrow. I see movement in its throat then what looks like a fine spray from bill's end, some gargly throat clearing before an operatic burst of song, its rapid, ribbon tongue unspooling to taste the air.

I left for Vermont, for a future unknown, and the thrill of escape eroded with every mile. Low-thrumming nerves morphed into fear, ballooning into terror after a sleepless night in a house full of strangers. He was a long day's drive away, but I was afraid. After thirteen years, I was leaving a man who'd once held a kitchen knife to my throat.

This is not a hostage story. Except that it is. And suddenly I want to apologize for being a cliché, for having these experiences, for not knowing better, for still feeling the effects. Which is to say I (still) want to apologize for being human.

Every morning I return to the rocks on the beach. I breathe slowly. I let the constant waves lull my brain: rest, rest, rest. I tell myself, *Don't think of the dead gull.* Which summons its image from the crypts of my mind. Okay, at least don't look for it. There, Mount Baker, snow-capped and stunning. There, mergansers, puffing their heads. The clouds shapeshift, sunlight burns distant but fierce, and I feel my life pulsing from every cell. Still, I look. I look until I see those pale legs. The dingy wing separating like a frayed hem. I never draw closer to look at the whole corpse, but I never sit on the other side of the rocks either. I hope that one morning I will not see any evidence of this fallen thing submerged and stuck between shore and sea.

We made dinner in his apartment one night in our first months together, his children gone visiting their mother. I was chopping lettuce when I felt him behind me, mouth warm on my ear. Then the thin, cool edge of his knife at my throat. My brain blanked. Love or danger? I froze, waiting to learn what to believe. He kissed my neck. He used that knife to finish preparing a romantic dinner for two.

I could not stay at the Vermont residency. Panicked and frantic, my brain wired for motion, I bolted, leaving one kind friend's house then another, weaving my way back to my children. I picked them up from daycare and called him. Choking with the shame of my vulnerability, this all-consuming distress, I told how I'd broken down, terrified, unable to stay. His words, little knives severing my last threads of hope: "Have you ruined my chances of going there now?"

I keep the evidence I need to remind myself of the nature of a relationship six years in the past and receding, but still punctuated with court filings and contemptuous messages, ugly exchanges over those children who I keep pressing to the far edges of this essay. Not forgetting, but protecting.

We lived apart for a year before I moved to join him. In one of our many emails, I wrote, "Danger is sexy. You've held a knife to my throat before." He confirmed this memory, adding, "I suppose I had a need to 'push' your trust in me to see if you really did trust me." Encouraged, I elaborated, recalling how I smiled and pressed my body back into his. But he insisted that he would have remembered that. No, he told me, you didn't smile or even flinch. "I thought you'd do *something*." But I froze and I waited. For thirteen years. Love or danger? When I finally tapped into that other possibility, I ran for my life.

There are still children darting along the edges of this story, children I leave behind for these necessary retreats. There is guilt and fear. Anger when I'm at his mercy to communicate with my children. Memories of him telling other children how their mother had abandoned them. The piled weight of his scorn and contempt followed by long, silent stretches that still say "you are dead (to me)." But, finally, too, there is my refusal to play dead.

One spring a student shared her writing teacher's favorite metaphor:
Love is a hummingbird with its throat cut. Another impressed student stole the line for a short story. I was sickened but careful in my response because I, too, had once been impressed. I'd craved the sugared rush of violent passion, terrorism packaged as some twisted test of trust and love. His knife, once at my throat, remained there for years, held by my own willing fingers.

I keep my promise to visit the beach every day. On the windy, rain-slicked morning that I don't see legs or wing when the tide pulls back, my heart seizes. If it's not there, where I expect to find something horrible, I don't know where or when I may be ambushed. I edge closer, wanting a glimpse. Nothing but the brutal, empty kisses of water and rock.

A gathering of hummingbirds is called a bouquet. A tune. A glittering. Or a charm. On my last morning on Orcas Island two hummingbirds frolic in the mist, luminous as light shattering water. When they pause to rest in a bare hydrangea, they rub their bills against the branch like whetstone. Staying sharp, staying ready. They will not be caged in hands, even gentle ones. They are no one's sacrifice, not even their own.

This essay was first published in the Blue Lyra Review

THE PANIC ATTACK OF A POET

by Rehana Campbell

It rises up through vulnerable temples,
Fizzing like a poured soda,
Taking a tour of an endless drop,
An ever-darkening ride to a past time.
Shit, I think,
My fingers seething with adrenaline,
A never-ending heart race,
Palpable like heartache.
I know what is to come,
And I am certain this is the uninvited guest.
Nevertheless, a trying defense, my mind mending fences:
If an open sea can carry its waves,
So can I and sleep soundly in graves.
I turn around to meet the fear,
One so dark depth disappears.
I am hurled through this vacuum,
Will it ever end? Desperation then thickly spreads,
Trapped in the pores of uneasing breads.
Just when my thoughts try to transcend,
A river of pain seeps out of my lens.

Don't worry, it will be over soon, a faraway thought suddenly reminds.

The words mix like water and oil,
Hopelessly stirring forever and ever.
The words mix like water and sugar,
Hopefully stirring for better and better.
The words mix like water and syrup,
A seamless stirring of thought and spirit.

This is a homecoming. You are here, and you are home.
There isn't anywhere you need to be, and there isn't anyone you need to see.
Your source of comfort is simply there, in you, for you, all the time.
It is unlimited, and it is specifically yours.
In no way does it impose on or interfere with your free will.
It is unconditional. It is you. It is love.

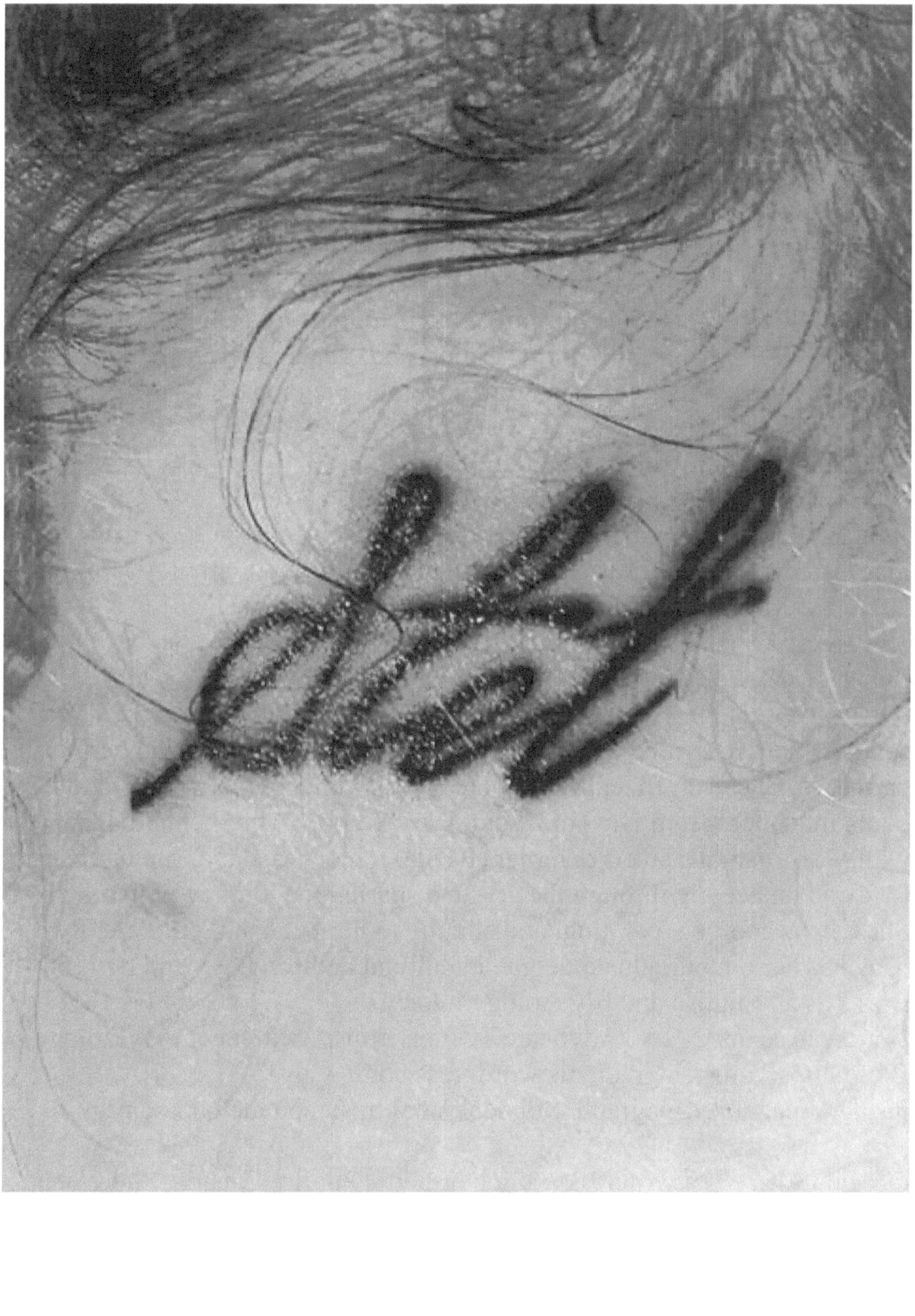

Meaghan Andrews is a Georgia-based writer with four poems having been previously published with *The Fall Line Review*. She also does editing.

Kelly Baker is an author and freelance writer located just north of Toronto. She enjoys reading and writing non-fiction. Her book is based on a true story that occurred in a small town in Pennsylvania. It's about a man who worked along side the hate crime division of the police department which helped to bring down a racist sister group of Aryan Nations and can be found at https://www.amazon.com/White- Supremacy-Behind-Eyes-Hate/dp/1412023548 Kelly lives with her husband, dog and guinea pigs. She enjoys writing, gardening, swimming, shooting pool and spending time with family and friends.
facebook.com/kelly.roberts.3760?fref=ts

Julie Butler is a Canadian writer whose essay, *Practising Grief*, was long-listed for the CBC "Canada Writes" Creative Nonfiction Award in 2016. Her work can be found at www.juliebutlerart.com.

Rehana Campbell is an artist based in Vancouver. *The Narcissist's Playbook* is the first publication of her poetry. Rehana is also involved with song-writing, recording, and music production. In 2015, she and her music partner produced an EP called "Good Vibes (with a grain of salt)" that harbours influences from Hip Hop, soul, jazz and pop. After being diagnosed with post-traumatic stress disorder (PTSD) a few years ago, she has been focusing on healing through the arts and sharing the journey with others. She enjoys cooking, painting, and singing to her pet fish, Petit Pete. Rehana has her undergraduate degree in cultural anthropology and currently works as an English and psychology tutor.
Goodreads.com/CPTSDAdvocate Twitter: https://twitter.com/HyFiology
Blog: https://musicingredients.wordpress.com/
instagram.com/rehanagraph/ Soundcloud: https://soundcloud.com/hy-fi

Oceania Chase is a writer based in Northern Ontario, Canada. She writes in a variety of genres, including pieces based on her personal life experiences, and is currently completing background research needed for her first novel. She can be contacted at oceaniachase@gmail.com.

Shay Cook earned an MFA in Creative Writing from National University and a Bachelor's in English from the University of Phoenix. She is the recipient of the Hillsborough County Lit Wit Poetry Contest, Winner of the Tampa Tribune Letter of the Day, and author of a collected work of poems entitled "Black Silk." Shay's poetry has appeared in both online and print venues. Her recent work has been published in *The GNU Journal, Mother's Always Write Magazine, Silver Birch Press,* and *Entropy Magazine*. Shay's nonfiction pieces have been published in Writer's World, Office Professional Magazine, Write Now, Chips Off the Writer's Block, Yesterday's Magazette, and numerous small presses and National publications. Shay is currently working on her second book of poetry, *A Pale Shade of Color*. In her spare time she hosts local creative writing workshops. Shay lives in Tampa, Florida.
goodreads.com/author/show/6583370.Shay_Cook
facebook.com/profile.php?id=100000530195324
Shaycook.org

Chauna Craig is the author of the story collection The *Widow's Guide to Edible Mushrooms* (Press 53, 2017). Her writing has appeared in *Ploughshares, Fourth Genre, Prairie Schooner, Crab Orchard Review* and other literary magazines and anthologies. She's received fellowships to Vermont Studio Center and Hedgebrook, and her work has been selected as a Notable Essay in Best American Essays and for Special Mention in the Pushcart Prize anthology. She teaches creative writing and women's studies at Indiana University of Pennsylvania.
chaunacraig.com
twitter.com/ChaunaCraig

Mo Daviau is the author of the novel *Every Anxious Wave*. Her nonfiction appears in *Nailed Magazine, The Toast,* and *The Offing*. She calls Portland, Oregon home, but has spent most of 2017 at an artist's colony in rural northern New England, finishing her second novel.
facebook.com/modaviau
twitter.com/modaviau
Goodreads: goodreads.com/author/show/14056216.Mo_Daviau

Kate Davis

Terri Elders, a retired licensed clinical social worker, is a lifelong writer and editor. After living and working all over the world, she recently

returned to settle in Southern California, where she remains active with the American Association of University Women and the Orange County Peace Corps Association. Her creative nonfiction pieces have been featured in over 100 books, including such series as *Chicken Soup for the Soul, A Cup of Comfort, Thin Threads,* and *HCI Ultimate*.
http://atouchoftarragon.blogspot.com/
amazon.com/Terri-Elders/e/B00CXYZ380

Ayesha Fayyaz is a young emerging poetess. She studies medicine and is also a member of International Association of Professional Writers and Editors. Her poems have appeared in *Elite Critique Magazine* and *Indiana Voice Journal*. She has also worked as a freelancer. She hopes to publish her debut anthology soon.

Jeanie Greensfelder is the author of *Biting the Apple* (Penciled In, 2012), and *Marriage and Other Leaps of Faith* (Penciled In, 2015). Her poems have been published at Writer's Almanac and American Life in Poetry; in anthologies: *Paris, Etc., Pushing the Envelope: Epistolary Poems, To Unsnare Time's Warp,* and *30 Years of Corner of the Mouth*; and in journals: *Askew, Miramar, Orbis, Kaleidoscope, Riptide, Solo Novo, Falling Star, If&When* and *others*. Poetry Awards: Lillian Dean and Spirit First. Jeanie Greensfelder grew up in St. Louis, Missouri. A psychologist, she seeks to understand herself and others on this shared journey, filled, as Joseph Campbell wrote, with sorrowful joys and joyful sorrows. Now living on the central coast of California with her husband Andy, she writes poetry.

Melissa Grossman is an active member of Paradigm Poets in Los Angeles, CA., as well as a member of the Ventura County performance troupe, Razor Babes. As a member of The Almost Famous Poets, she brings poetry to the Ventura County Schools. Her poetry has been published in *Common Ground Review, Askew, Kansas City Voices*, the anthology *In the Company of Women*, and two Lucid Moose anthologies: *Alleyways & Gutters: Poverty & Struggle* and *Like a Girl*. Melissa is a stained glass and mosaic artist, living in Simi Valley with her beloved Golden Retriever, Molly.
melissagrossman.com

Julie Guirgis' writing has appeared in several publications including *The Aquarian, Back Home, Eureka St, Signs of the Times, Adventist review, Creation Illustrated, Madonna, Majellan, Now What?, The Edge, Guide, Insight, Kaleidoscope, Transition*, and more. Links to some of her work

can be found on:
eurekastreet.com.au/article.aspx?aeid=49521#V33AuaKlj3i
adventistreview.org/1601-32
edgemagazine.net/2015/10/coconut-oil-in-a-nutshell/

Jolene Hughes is finding herself through words and other art. She can be contacted at jolenehughes@gmail.com.

Beth Jordan

Erin Laing graduated from the Mel Hoppenheim School of Cinema in 2003 and has actively been working in the film industry since. She has a passion for writing, be it screenplays, poetry, fiction or non-fiction. Her short films have screened in film festivals all over the world and have won awards including the grand prize for *Cours Ecrire Ton Court!*, a major Quebec screenwriting competition. Her most recent short film *Timber* is currently doing the festival circuit, and she is in development on her first feature film titled *Wall of Sound.*
Birthday Girl: https://vimeo.com/72058961

Bella Lord is an English major at UC Davis with an emphasis in creative writing.

J. Kathleen Marcus is a lawyer who writes, and a fiber artist who spins raw wool. She grew up in New York City and isn't sure how many step-fathers she had. Marcus was the most junior lawyer on the trial team of *Planned Parenthood v. Casey* (helping to fight back an overturn of *Roe v. Wade*) when she was 26 and was Politics Editor at *Mothering* magazine in her late 40's. She is the nation's foremost expert on breastfeeding legislation (quoted in, among other publications, *The New York Times, Washington Post, Newsweek*) and can pull Romney fleece curls until only the need to pee makes her stop. Marcus lives in the Philadelphia suburbs with her three adult-ish children. She also lives with major autoimmune disorders and is in chronic pain.
jakemarcus.com

Linda Maxwell is a high school English teacher who also contributes free-lance articles for the *Georgetown Times* in Georgetown, South Carolina. She has published poetry in *The Chaffin Journal, The Southern Women's Review* and *Wordriver*. Visit her at facebook.com/linda.g.maxwell

Sarah Miner is a life and business coach, writer, artist, athlete, publisher, and mother of three. She wrote and illustrated *The Wind Whispered Her Name*, a feminist fairy tale allegory of domestic and narcissistic abuse, a portion of which she read at the Unchaste Readers Series in Portland, Oregon. Her coaching practice focuses on shifting people and businesses out of crisis.
skminer.com
Facebook.com/skminercoaching

Molly Pennington writes essays and commentary on social justice, popular culture, feminism and parenting. She holds a PhD from the University of Pittsburgh where her research focused on masculinity and race in presidential politics.
MollyPennington.com
Facebook.com/mollypenningtonphd
Twitter.com/docpennington

Kathryn Peterson is the author of "Split Happens," a column on separation, divorce and relationships that ran weekly on the Houston Chronicle's blog for almost two years. She holds a Ph.D. and MFA in fiction from the University of Houston, and an M.A. in playwriting from the University of Cincinnati. She is currently writing a literary suspense novel titled *A Perfect Room for Sleeping* and owns her own business, consulting with writers on theses, dissertations and a variety of creative projects. She also works with writers in the K-12 environment through the Houston-based nonprofit organization Writers in the Schools.

Kristen Polito is a writer based in Florida. You can read her public blog, Salt and Pepper The Earth at www.saltandpepperthearth.com, follow her on twitter @saltandpepperth, facebook, or visit her author page here on Amazon.

Jo Rider is a writer from Portland Oregon, and this is her writing debut.

Amy Oestreicher is a PTSD peer-to-peer specialist, artist, author, writer for Huffington Post, speaker for TEDx and RAINN, health advocate, survivor, award-winning actress, and playwright, sharing the lessons learned from trauma through her writing, mixed media art, performance and inspirational speaking. As the creator of Gutless & Grateful, her BroadwayWorld-nominated one-woman autobiographical musical, she's toured

theaters nationwide, along with a program combining mental health advocacy, sexual assault awareness, and Broadway Theatre for college campuses and international conferences. She has studied as a playwright and performance artist in the National Musical Theatre Institute at the world-renowned Eugene O'Neill Theater Center. Her original, full-length drama, Imprints, premiered at the NYC Producer's Club in May 2016, exploring how trauma affects the family as well as the individual. To celebrate her own "beautiful detour", Amy created the #LoveMyDetour campaign, to help others cope in the face of unexpected events. "Detourism" is also the subject of her TEDx and upcoming book, *My Beautiful Detour*, available December 2017. As Eastern Regional Recipient of Convatec's Great Comebacks Award, she's spoken to hundreds of healthcare professionals at national WOCN conferences, and her presentations on diversity, leadership, and trauma have been featured at National Mental Health America Conference, New England Educational Opportunity Association's 40th Anniversary Conference, and have been keynotes at the Pacific Rim Conference of Diversity and Disability in Hawaii and the Eating Recovery Foundation First Annual Benefit in Colorado. She's contributed to over 70 notable online and print publications, and her story has appeared on NBC's TODAY, CBS, and Cosmopolitan, among others.
amyoes.com.

Catherine Wald's chapbook, *Distant, burned-out stars*, was published by Finishing Line Press in 2011. Poems have appeared in *American Journal of Nursing, Buddhist Poetry Review, Chronogram, Friends Journal, J Journal, Jewish Literary Journal, The Lyric, Minerva Rising, The New York Times,* and *Westchester Review*, among others. She is author of *The Resilient Writer: Tales of Triumph and Rejection from 23 Top Authors* (Persea 2004).
CatherineWald.com

Mandy Waysman is a blogger, wife, and mom to two daughters. You can find her work on the *Huffington Post, Scary Mommy, In The Powder Room, BonBon Break, humorwriters.org, Sammiches & Psych Meds*, and other parenting sites. She has more personality than this bio would lead you to believe. For proof please follow her as she becomes a regular contributor on http://www.losethecape.com and her current blog ohmandelynn.com
facebook.com/ohmandelynn
twitter.com/OhMandelynn

Debbie Weingarten is a freelance writer based in Tucson, Arizona. Her writing has appeared in *Guernica, Vela, Aeon, The Development Set, Terrain.org, The Establishment, Modern Farmer, Civil Eats*, and others, as well as the *2016 Best of Food Writing* anthology. She is a regular features contributor for *Edible Baja Arizona* and a writing partner for the Female Farmer Project.
Cactuswrenwriting.com.